Dr Break Through Overcomes Limiting Beliefs

By the time you are finished reading and implementing the principles in this book, you'll be breaking through seemingly impossible things as well!

NOTICE

DISCLAIMER

For questions or comments concerning this book, please send an email to DrBreakTo@gmail.com or 717MrsHarris@gmail.com

To book Dr. Break Through to do a tele-conference or speak for your business, team, school or church please call (717) 275-3508.

Dr Break Through Publishing
Frisco, Texas
DrBreakTo@gmail.com

DEDICATION

I want to dedicate this book to four powerful Woman who have influenced my life in a profound way. They are like the four legs that hold up a chair and make it sturdy.

Imagine also a building with four pillars supporting the structure, or as they say in Texas, "If you see a Turtle on a post, you know he didn't get there by himself."

The first pillar was my grandmother Daisy Stewart who passed away when I was young but who left memories that I will cherish for the rest of my life. She was the glue that kept the extended family together. She was simply amazing, literally a saint.

The second was my precious mom Thelma Jean Gessler who inspired me to learn Martial Arts, who taught me a work ethic and many other great lessons with her life. She believed in me and let me know she was proud of me many times before she passed away June 19th 1991. By the way, she was the same age I am now which is only 49.

The third pillar is my daughter Christina Harris who I refer to as my baby girl. Watching her birth changed my life, and she has believed in me and it's hard to explain, but she evokes the greatness in me to surface. I love you so much and am so proud of you. Baby girl you will always have a special place in my heart. Once when I was at my lowest and suicidal, I continued on because of your belief in me.

And last but not least, my sweet brown cinnamon sugar, Nadia MeChelle who makes me feel like I can conquer the world. Your sweet, quiet, and gentle spirit turns me on and moves me to become more. You are the wind beneath my wings and I love you and pray daily that God would love you through me! I love traveling with you, and enjoy writing, walking and talking with you. You are my Queen, you possess charm and wit, sexiness and spirituality you are my best friend, and I honor you. You are a great wife, mother, daughter, writer, etc. and the world will one day soon hear your almost unbelievable story!

Dedicated family man even when caught off guard

Dr Stan breaking 22 inches of burning cement block with his bare hands!

ACKNOWLEDGMENTS

I humbly thank my LORD for without Him and His grace, none of this would be possible. All Scripture quotations are from the King James Bible.

I want to especially thank Stephen and Alicia Pierce as well as some of their staff like Chipo Mudzengi who supported me whole heartedly during this project.

Thank you Myron Golden my mentee/mentor for your help with this project and I want to thank the students of the Six Figure Business School (Dallas class) who supported me, and purchased my book before it was finished!

Thanks to my brothers Keith, Ronald, and Lonnie (Daniel) for writing such powerful endorsements. Also thanks to my Daughter Christina and my three Sons Joshua, Josiah, and Justin for honoring me with your kind words, I cannot wait to read your books one day soon! I am humbled by your giftedness and greatness.

Thanks Brenda Stroman for calling this work "a Masterpiece" and for helping with proofreading and editing along with Joyce Barrie and Christina Harris.

I want to thank you the reader for opening yourself up to learn how to tap into your hidden or suppressed Break Through power and to create new possibilities for yourself!

A special shout out to the photographers who captured some incredible shots: Bill Mitchell and Sylvia Dunnavant.

In closing, thanks to the teamwork of Chad Haycox at Country Pines Printing and Mike McCoy at M&K Publishing for their invaluable assistance!

Eating Fire

Eat your fears before they eat you!

TABLE OF CONTENTS

Why People Who Know Dr Stan Best Believe You Should Purchase And Read His Powerful Book

"Only read this book if you want a Guaranteed Break Through! If you are tired of a life of struggle and disappointment, and your looking to experience life at a new level, *Your Break Through is Guaranteed* will be one of the most important books of your life. Having known Dr Stan for over 33 years and having witnessed the Break Throughs he has experienced, I admonish you to allow this Break Through Grand Master to lead you to the Break Through you've been longing and looking for."

Myron Golden
Trainer, Author and Entrepreneur

"When my father first asked me to write an endorsement for his book, I declined. I was busy working and hadn't had time to read the book, and didn't feel that I should write an endorsement for something I hadn't read. Well since then things have definitely changed! Because of some personal issues in my life, I made time to read his book, and I am so glad that I did! This book is one of the most powerful things I've ever read (and I've read literally hundreds, perhaps thousands of books). Buying this book for yourself or a loved one is an investment that will allow the reader to reap numerous, multi-faceted rewards. I can personally guarantee from experience that if you implement the principles within this book, you will experience a break through in one or more areas of your life."

Christina Harris, Daughter
English Teacher, Editor

"Why should you read this book? I have three reasons for you that tell why I would read his book:

1) What he has gone through and what he has become in -spite- of it. The man doesn't know the meaning of "product of the environment," instead he is the very definition of rising above the environment.

2) His King David walk with God.

3) His ability to put up with my incessant questions, occasional capriciousness, and Herculean stubbornness, all the while helping to mold a man and a Marine through it all (me).

"I learned to talk with God from the way that he walks with God. I learned to walk with God by the way that he trusts God. I learned to trust God by the way that he lives for God. And I learned to set an example by simply striving for his."

To my dad: "It is an honor to be the oldest son of one of the great Kings of our time."

To everyone else: "I have seen him go from a brand new Lincoln Navigator and Motor Home, to no car and then back to luxury vehicles. He has gone from flash and fire to fire and substance to Vessel of the Spirit, from burnout and back again.

"He has been more than I can keep track of, and done more than I hope to ever have to go through. I promise you that you will not be disappointed."

Joshua S. Harris (Oldest Son)
Sgt. US Marine Served Two tours to Afghanistan

"Many of you are probably thinking like I was when I first heard my dad talking about his breakthrough concept "What the heck are you talking about?" He would incessantly fill my ear with tales of people whose lives had been changed. I would congratulate him but distance myself from his many business ventures, all the while hoping for a financial breakthrough of my own. Big mistake! I believe my first hands-on experience with a Dr. Stan Harris "breakthrough" came when I was in the 12th grade. He told me about this company that was built around pay-per-click advertising; the amounts of money he was saying I could make seemed all too good to be true. So being the skeptic that I tend to be most of the time, I received the concept with large amounts of incredulism. $7,000 and my first car later, I had to concede that he might have found his niche after all.

"I now believe that breakthroughs are real and when you work with my dad, they pretty much seem inevitable. I've now produced a cd entitled *Lyrics of the Heart* and have a book already put together called *Don't Call Me a Poet* that I'm waiting to publish.

"Don't wait like I did, the time for your breakthrough is **now!**"

A1C Josiah J. Harris, Son
USAF Boom Operator

"My father Dr. Stan Harris has a dynamic wealth of knowledge in business, public speaking, spirituality and life in general. At the healthy age of 49 his traveling and speaking engagements rival Presidents. He has spoken around the world, and his network is vast.

"Do you like someone who is electrifying and animated? Do you want to know how to get out of the norm and experience opportunities you are passing up without even thinking about? Then read his book, every day is a new experience and with each new experience, opportunity is close by. Motivate yourself to invest in your future, your mind and growth in these times of economic hardships.

"Think of his book as an appendage to your future, after all two heads are better than one. A great poet once said, "Ingenuity is like a hermit crab, it tries on people until it finds the one that fits." Conform around ingenuity and success has already happened."

Justin M. Harris, Youngest Son
18 years old

"This awesome book, *Your Breakthrough is Guaranteed* is a must read. It is a practical guide to reaching goals by using 7 simple steps to ensure that your breakthrough is guaranteed. Dr. Stan teaches ageless Biblical principles that reveal the keys to personal development and success.

"Dr. Stan 'Breakthrough' Harris has a remarkable gift for motivating and moving people to take the necessary actions to move into their (GREATNESS) desired place of total freedom in every area of their life. He has the ability to articulate his beliefs in such a way that captivates and galvanizes the audience.

"This book demonstrates strategies, tactics, and engaging accounts from his life experiences. As Dr. Stan's wife, guess what question I'm asked constantly? Is he like this all the time? The answer is Yes! My husband is always full of energy, excited about the future, and excited about life.

"One thing that I love so much about him, he is the same in public as he is in private, a man of integrity and character. He is a man who is spiritually grounded very transparent and loves educating and empowering people. As my husband would say, It's the start that stops most people, don't let the start stop you. Get this book today."

Nadia Harris, Wife
a.k.a. Lady BreakThrough

"This Book is Epic in scope comparable to Dr. Stan himself. You see I know him personally, he happens to be my brother. Although he is my younger brother, he has impacted my life and empowered me to experience Break Throughs in my health, spirituality, relationships and finances. This book is both enthralling & captivating in its integrity which reflects my brother's character. The words therein form an esoteric union with the reader that is second to none.

"Stan, our grandmother would be so proud of you, as I and the rest of the family are."

Waddell K Stewart, Brother
Computer Consultant/Developer/Enthusiast

"Dr. Stan Harris also known as Dr Break Through, has the prescription and breakthrough principals that will allow you to see who you really are. He's an amazing speaker, leader and teacher. Read this book, and you will be forced to break-through your own barriers in life. This book is a must-read for people of all walks of life. Thank you Dr. Stan Harris for sharing your gifts with the world. It's a better place because you showed up!"

Tawana Williams
Motivational Speaker/Author and CEO

"Dr. Stan Harris is a very powerful Breakthrough expert that everyone needs to be exposed to. If you need a Breakthrough in your mind, self-esteem, health, wealth, career, etc. read this book. If you want your life to really soar knock on the Dr.'s Break Through Door!"

Anthony Stroman, Motivational Speaker & CEO

"After 81 years of life, my goal is to make for a better world, and if ever there was a book to do that, it is this one!"

Beryl Wolk
World's Greatest Marketing Genius

"My nephew has always inspired me. His wit, wisdom and speaking changes lives and you would do well to read his book. He really walks his talk and he is a man passionate about changing lives. Allow him to change yours."

Robert L. Stewart, Uncle

"Dr. Stan Harris; You are a man on a mission! To have a vision is good, to share your vision is better, but to spread your vision is by far the best. To take the common and make it uncommon and to take the ordinary and make it extraordinary is a unique talent very few people posses.

"The ultimate measure of a man is not what he has achieved but what he has overcome. Dr. Harris is a survivor and an over comer of the highest order.

"When he speaks people listen and lives are changed. His book *Your Breakthrough is Guaranteed* will stretch your thoughts expand your mind broaden your vision and enlarge your dreams beyond your wildest imagination."

Basketball Bill Chaffin, Speaker/Author
Guinness Book Of World Records **Holder**

"This is one for the shelves!!! You have got to pick up your copy of Dr. Stan's new book and grasp the wisdom and knowledge this guy possesses! I have known Stan for about 47 years and he is amazing. He is a man of God, a successful Entrepreneur, Grand Master Martial Artist, worldwide Motivational/Break Through speaker, dedicated husband, father and genuine person.

"His ability to articulate and communicate publicly is unprecedented. When I heard him speak, I was in awe. I've only touched on a few key points of his abilities and knowledge. I could go on for hours discussing this native born Pennsylvanian, but I think I'd rather not spoil it for you.

Get his book for yourself, a loved one and/or a friend. I assure you of enlightenment throughout each chapter!

"It has been a true honor to know my big brother and I am truly proud of his accomplishments past and present, as well as what he will achieve in the future.

"If you had a big 'Brother' like my brother 'Stan' you would be proud as well. I'll see you all in chapter one of *Your Break Through Is Guaranteed.*

Daniel L. Harris, Sr., Younger Brother
U.S. Army, (Retired) Operation Iraq Freedom
2006-Present

"You may wonder, 'Why this book, what makes this book any different or special?' The book is special, because the man is special! I have personally witnessed this my whole life (48 years). There is a God-given gift this man possesses and he wants to share it with the world. Even though we all have it, we need the key to unlock our power, perseverance, and spirituality. This book is the key."

Your younger brother,
Ronald K. Harris

"Wow, awesome, fabulous are just a few words that came to mind when I read just a portion of this powerful book. As a host of the largest Home Based Business Radio Show, we have had Dr Break Through on our show more than any other guest! I also have a daily call where I read a part of this book every day to my team members.

"This man has wisdom like few people I have encountered, you must get his book(s), attend his seminars etc. The man is a go-getter and he motivates people to do more than they ever dreamed possible. Dr Break Through is like a rock star, but even more, he makes you feel like a star!"

Tom Chenault
The Home Based Business Radio Show

When Dr. Stan speaks I stop and listen. His teachings are now available to YOU, the lucky reader through his book *Your Breakthrough is Guaranteed.*

The steps he walks through in this book will help YOU to experience a breakthrough in your life. As I read the book, I took pages of notes. As you read chapter 3 on facts, please highlight this sentence "The greatest things in life are still awaiting your arrival." Isn't that powerful?

When you read chapter 12 – you will be set free. You'll be set free from yourself and the negative talk in your head. Dr. Stan's powerful quote in this chapter is "We are reaping what we have sown by having what we have said. If you'd like a different harvest, get busy planting different seeds."

Dr. Stan, I would just like to thank you for the gift of your years of experience condensed in this awesome book. To YOU, the reader, I'm writing this after the first printing of this book, and having known that it's already changed lives, I'm excited for YOUR life to change after reading this book.

I'd like you to do me a favor. After you've read this book, buy another copy for that person in your life that needs a break-through! They'll thank you for it.

Alicia Pierce
Speaker, Trainer, Internet Entreprenuer

FOREWORD

I once heard that you can't have a breakthrough without having a breakdown. I have to say I believe this truth with all my heart. Now, by breakdown, I don't mean that you have to be institutionalized necessarily but rather that for real transformation to take place, most of us have to get to a place of acute honesty about our shortcomings and our participation in a life of mediocrity.

If you're truly committed to a life of extreme and sustainable success, you'll likely have many breakthroughs...and breakdowns. I certainly have. As an elite athlete and now national television personality, I am faced with challenges I didn't even know existed. Show business can be an incendiary and crazy place sometimes. And I have to remind myself that fame and fortune, while fun and exciting, if not put in proper perspective, can lead to your ruin.

So, I have a strict policy: I must have at least one major breakthrough every 30 days in some area of my life. And because I have that level of expectancy, guess what happens? Yes, like clockwork I have my breakdowns and breakthroughs!

When I heard that Dr. Stan was writing *Your Breakthrough Is Guaranteed,* a guide based on his revolutionary teachings and breakthrough principles, I got very excited. Now of course when I first encountered Dr. Stan many years ago I, like many of you, was mesmerized by his passion and command of his topic, but I was more impressed that he was willing to share his very personal story and breakthrough journey.

You see, it's one thing to stand before thousands of people and proclaim to be the expert or "guru" but it's quite another thing to stand before your peers and acknowledge that the road to your unique greatness hasn't exactly been a picnic.

And that's why I have such admiration for Dr. Stan and the work he's doing to help people.

He's not simply spouting off anecdotes, he's showing us how his principles live and breathe, creating next-level living for those who choose to participate in their own break though and transformation.

What started out as a journey to protect himself as a young boy, has become a masterful teaching tool. Sure, being a Black Belt Champion is cool but in my view, his crowning achievement lies in the fact that he's written a book that beautifully demonstrates the connection between his discipline as an athlete and teacher, and the core principles for success.

Your Breakthrough Is Guaranteed will, no doubt, challenge you. It will inspire you and it will ignite you. So, if you're truly ready for a life beyond your imagination, make it your business to read this book immediately. It will put you on the fast track to a lifetime of breakthroughs and victories. Guaranteed!

Fran Harris
WNBA Champion & Host of HGTV's "Home Rules"
www.FranHarris.com

Fran Harris & Dr Stan Harris (not related)

Dr. Stan is highly regarded as an icon of transformation, helping thousands of people dramatically expand their lives and manifest their greatness.

We all come to a point in our lives where we feel stuck, unable to move forward. As a young person, and before I became a speaker, I was stuck. I knew there was more that I could do but for some reason I could not move forward. It was my mentor, Mike Williams, who helped me find my Breakthrough and reach my true potential. This book by Dr. Stan can help you do the same.

This is a book that helps you make mental, emotional and physical changes on a cellular level in order to transform yourself and your life from the inside out. With his use of metaphors and examples from his experiences as a top level, martial arts expert, Dr Stan engages and inspires readers to challenge their belief systems, face their fears and to become risk takers.

More than hope and inspiration, *Your Breakthrough Is Guaranteed* offers a template, a roadmap that will help you move past your previous blocks in every area of your life and finally have the Breakthroughs you deserve.

If you are ready to take control of your life, if you are ready to improve your relationships, heal your heart, and reach your full potential, then you are ready for a Breakthrough. Dr. Stan's book, *Your Breakthrough Is Guaranteed* will take you there.

Les Brown
Motivational Speaker, Speech Coach, Author
www.lesbrown.com

This Book Will Change Your Life, Especially When You Implement These Simple Principles!

1. **Get a Book Buddy.** Ask another person to read the same book and become your learning and accountability partner.

2. **Respond and participate.** The more you respond and put in; the more you will get out, the less you respond and put in, the less you get out of the book.

3. **Underline and make notes** have a pen and highlighter handy. Underlining specific lines and paragraphs will triple your retention rate. Write your own thoughts in the margins and own this book. Write what you intend to do about certain principles.

4. **Re-read what you underlined.** Re-read your key items over and over. Record and listen to your notes while driving in your car. We often need to hear something several times before it sinks in.

5. **Apply the material immediately.** Doing so will help you understand the material better. Don't try to be perfect. Accomplishing something is better than trying to be perfect.

6. **Prioritizing what you want to implement.** Select one to three things from the book, apply them faithfully.

7. **Read this book more than once.** I've read certain books over and over again. The more you read a book the more you become like the book. One man read this book four times in one month! He is a successful network marketer (that might be a clue). A Billionaire told me he read a book 80 times thus far! He reads that book every year and many times, several times in a year!

8. **Share what you are learning with others.** By teaching others what you are learning causes you to grasp and learn more. Following these eight tips will help you turn this information into habits that will change your life! Let's get started right now!

Meet Dr. Stan "Break Through" Harris

Dr. Stan Harris
(a.k.a.) Dr. Break Through

(Doctorate of Divinity, Martial Arts, and a few credits away from his Doctorate of Naturopath) Dr. Stan Harris is perhaps the most entertaining, enlightening, and electrifying speaker on the circuit today. At age six, he was jumped, beaten, tarred and feathered by a teenage gang. He began martial arts to learn how to protect himself, and now, 41 years later, he is one of a few who has attained the highest honors of 10th Degree Black Belt, Grand Master (Isshin'ryu Karate). He has been inducted into the Black Belt Hall of Fame and the Motivational Speakers Hall of Fame. He is married to Nadia-MeChelle, the woman of his dreams. They have four children.

He has driven over two million miles using a combination of martial art skills and his energetic speaking ability to move crowds as large as 17,000, speaking in all 50 states and 27 countries.

As one of fewer than a hundred 10th degree black belts in the world, Dr. Harris delivers positive and empowering breakthrough messages as a motivational or Break Through speaker to people across the world.

Dr. Stan has shared the platform with the top speakers of the world and has co-authored several books with people like; Donald Trump, Chuck Norris, Brian Tracy, Suze Orman, Robert Kiyosaki, Jack Canfield, Les Brown, Bob Proctor, Loral Langemeier, T. Harv Eker, Wayne Dyer, Dan Kennedy, Zig Ziglar, Jim Rohn, Dr. Deepak Chopra, & Denis Waitley.

Dr. Stan says, "This book and my website are tools that are dedicated to helping you Break Through to the success that you desire and deserve. I invite you to visit my websites for more information and I look forward to seeing you at one of my seminars, hearing you on one of my tele-seminars, and perhaps having you as one of my coaching clients."

The image below **(It is time for me to break free!)** is the best visual picture of what this book will do for your mind and life. Things are keeping you back from being free to do what you were created to do.

It is time to break free from whatever binds you, so you can be free to be your authentic self. The world is waiting to meet the authentic you. Do not keep them waiting. When you meet the authentic you, it may shock you, because you are so much more than you realize.

As my gift to you, I have enclosed two $997 tickets to my world-famous Break Through Summit. This is a $1,994 value, absolutely free. This is my investment into your success. **This book comes with a 100% Money back Guarantee!**

Kindest regards,

Dr. Stan Harris

Dr. Stan Harris (a.k.a.) Dr. Break Through

It is time for me to break free!

www.JoinDrBreakThrough.com

PART I:

THE FOUNDATION

Congratulations on embarking upon your Break Through journey. I want to thank you for purchasing this book. I want to share my story with you, because my life is all about breakthroughs and assisting people in breaking through to the success that they desire and deserve.

At the young age of 3, my dad left home, never to return. Mom moved from Baltimore, Maryland up to Harrisburg, Pennsylvania, where we resided in government housing, commonly known as the projects or ghettos.

I remember waking in the middle of the night because I sensed something on my face. I slapped my face and shockingly found out that it was a giant cockroach. The whole place proved to be infested with roaches and rats. What would prove to be even worse were the drugs, crime and violence.

I will never forget when as a 6-year-old boy, playing in the middle of a field, I noticed a gang of teenagers approaching. I was so afraid, in essence, I was paralyzed by my fear.

They grabbed me and began punching me in the stomach. I fell to the ground in excruciating pain, gasping for air, wanting to breathe yet unable to catch my breath.

By the way, have you ever had the air knocked out of you? It's something you can't forget.

While I was on the ground, they punched me all over my body. They kicked and stomped on me until I was a bloody mess. Imagine being stomped upon as if you were an ant or cockroach! You would think the bullying would have stopped at this point, but never in my worst nightmare did I ever imagine what would happen next.

They flipped me over and poured a big bucket of tar all over my face and body. Then they threw feathers all over me and just left me there. I cried out for help during the attack, but like some big cities, nobody stopped to help.

Finally, somebody found me and rushed me to the hospital.

Thank God, the tar wasn't too hot, but it was thick. In fact, I almost suffocated. Finally, I had some relief.

I remember wondering, "Why would it take a gang of teenagers to beat up a 6-year-old boy?" I may never know the answer, but I have learned that people who have been hurt, tend to hurt others. Simply stated, "hurt people, sometimes, hurt people."

Back to my story, my little mind could not figure out some things, so I came to some conclusions. I concluded that, "something must be wrong with me." I also felt like no one cared about me (other than my mom).

I remember thinking, "My dad doesn't care. He never comes by. He never calls. He never sends Mom any money to help raise us."

I then reasoned, "Society doesn't care; they beat, tarred and feathered me."

A few years later, I received a beating with a steel choker chain. I was beat across my back and head with a steal folding chair by my mom's boyfriend.

I remember getting to the place of total despair. With tears flowing down my face, I remember going into the kitchen, grabbing a razor-sharp butcher knife and thinking, "I'm just going to kill myself; no one cares what happens to me anyway."

I made a mistake, I put the razor-sharp butcher knife on my belly button and I tried to pull it nice and slow. Well, that idea did not work. The knife only went in about a quarter of an inch, before I quickly dropped it on the ground. I was bleeding a little, screaming in pain I thought, "There has to be an easier way to kill myself, the knife hurts too much."

I had watched a television program that showed a man that was high on drugs who thought he was a bird. Sadly enough he jumped from the top of a building to his death. I got an idea and thought, "I'll jump off the top of the house, it will be fast, and I can't chicken out half way down."

I went to the top floor of the house, put my foot on the ledge of the window and planned to jump.

I started crying and saying to myself, "No one cares about you, just kill yourself; life is not worth living."

I was going to jump, but once I took a long look, down to the ground I gasped and said, "Oh, my goodness! If I jump down there I'll splash to pieces." Looking back, I am so glad I chickened out and did not jump!

I am sad to say, there are many people who have taken that leap, who have jumped, pulled the trigger, etc. They destroyed what was left of their lives by committing suicide. Thousands of people are contemplating suicide. I want to give them hope, and I desire to empower them so they can experience a break through. It has been aptly stated that, "Suicide is a permanent solution to a temporary problem."

I am telling you, my life was a wreck; it was a mess. Yet today, my life has totally changed. I want you to know that your life can be as well, and I am dedicated to assisting you in experiencing a break through.

I will never forget the day when my mother won a free month of Karate lessons. I went with her and watched. She liked it and stayed in the class. Even after her free month ran out she was so serious, she paid the monthly fee. Free is good, but you know people are serious when they are willing to pay with money they earned.

My Mom worked out very hard. I would watch, and she became what I jokingly call "too good."

If you wonder what I mean by the term "too good," let me explain. My Mom and her boyfriend got into a fight; she hit him in the jaw with a "side snap kick" and knocked him out cold!

I looked at my younger brothers Ronald, and Lonnie, we all looked at the person on the ground, and I remember saying, "Man! Whatever you do, do not mess with my mama. Because my mama is bad, Man, My mama's bad." (I now have two additional brothers, Keith and Shawn.)

I thought, "This is the secret. This is the answer. If I take this Martial Arts stuff, this Karate, I can learn how to protect myself. The next time somebody jumps me, I can protect myself. I can become a champion and people will finally care about me."

I remember going to Karate practice and working out. In that, I found something that changed my life forever. Now, some forty-one years later, out of almost seven billion people in the world, I am a 10th Degree Black Belt, which means I am one of the youngest Grand Masters.

I just retired a few years ago as the Heavyweight Champion with the Karate World rating system, and I have had some amazing success in my life. I was inducted into the Black Belt Hall of Fame, and I have also been inducted into the Motivational Speakers Hall of Fame. I've traveled all over the world to all 50 states and 27 countries, teaching and encouraging people to break through to the success that they desire and they deserve.

I have had some success in business, especially in the home based business industry, where I have been one of the top leaders in six different companies.

I remember a time during my fifth week in a new business that I had earned $9,563 for the week. By the time I got to my eighth week in that particular business, I had a check for a whopping $16,541.

That was for one week's worth of work. I have had the privilege to build a network marketing team to 22,826 people in only six short months (www.BuildABigTeamFast.com).

Imagine making a six-figure income, on a monthly basis! That is one reason why I love the home based business industry. It's the only place I know, where an average person can make above average income in below average time. I have even seen people with below average education, make above average income.

Again, I have experienced tremendous success. Just the other day I assisted a friend and business partner get a private label deal on his book. The company purchased 100,000 copies. We walked out of the office a few hours later with a check for $200,000. The remaining $200,000 will be collected in a few weeks upon completion of the project.

I served as a College professor for several years, and I enjoyed teaching self defense, African-American history, biographies of great men, public speaking, etc.

During the summer, I traveled full time with my beautiful family in our motor home. My children were home schooled or perhaps it is best to say road schooled. (smile)

Standing:
Joshua, Dr. Stan

Sitting:
Justin, Christina, and
Josiah Harris

I have four beautiful children. Christina is the oldest and is a high school teacher working on her master's degree. Recently, I spoke for her school and she said, "Dad, when I get my doctorate, we're going to both be 'Dr. Harris' (she's still single) and I would like us to write a book together." Recently, Christina successfully created and wrote the curriculum for an African American literature course for the Susquehanna Township School District in Pennsylvania.

Joshua is in the Marines and has served two tours in Afghanistan defending our country. He desires to become a college professor.

Josiah is an unbelievable poet. I have had him on the platform with me several times and crowds love his poetry. He serves in the Air Force and plans to attend college upon completion of his assignment. Justin is the youngest. He plays football and is a hard worker. He plans to attend college after high school.

My wife Nadia is my soul/spirit mate. In my opinion, she is the most beautiful, smartest, sexiest, soft-spoken woman in the world. She has authored six books, and we are writing a book together. We love to travel and work together. Her very essence brings the best out of me.

I just sealed a seven figure business deal the other day!

However, life was not always this way…

People ask me from time to time, "How in the world did you get from where you were to where you are now?" That, my friend, is called a breakthrough.

Many people talk about breakthroughs, very few experience them. This book, my life, and my coaching are dedicated to help you break through to your success, however you define success! I am going to assist you by giving you my seven-step breakthrough formula that will assist you in breaking through any barrier that would hinder your success.

Several barriers hinder people from reaching their desired success. I will talk about some of the barriers that I had to break through and some things that you will have to break through. As I travel the country, both nationally and internationally, I assist people in breaking through barriers.

Here is a quick thought: *"Barriers were not made to stop you. Barriers were made to be broken."* My definition of a breakthrough is *exploding through barriers that at one time seemed insurmountable.* The operative word is the word seemed. All that I do presently seemed impossible to me years ago.

I tell people, "I'm the world's first breakthrough speaker, which is different than motivation. Motivation is good, but it is like a shower. You have to have one every day, and sometimes twice a day." A breakthrough is far beyond that.

Most motivational speakers are good, for an example, they would motivate a caterpillar to move a little faster. Would you be inclined to agree that caterpillar needs to move a lot faster? Well, of course...

However, as a breakthrough speaker, I assist the caterpillar into the cocoon, and then out of the cocoon as a beautiful butterfly. It is a total life transformation. I use motivation, inspiration, education, entertainment, and oftentimes a Martial Arts demonstration to help assist a person in breaking through to the next level. What we hear, we tend to forget. What we see, we tend to remember. However, what we experience, we never forget. I made this book interactive to create experiences that you will never forget. With this in mind, may I request you become a participator and not a spectator, get involved and respond aloud when I ask, okay? I did not hear you. (smile) I am constantly seeking to grow and experience greater Break Throughs.

Part of what motivates me to help others by writing this book, creating seminars, CD's/DVD's and coaching programs, is simple, when I help others, I get helped myself.

I have a seven-step Break Through formula, but you may be only one-step from a massive Break Through! Are you ready to learn and apply this simple formula?

By the way, your very DNA is coded genetically to experience Break Throughs. I will prove it to you quickly. Your conception was your first breakthrough. The second was when your mother's water broke and you broke through the womb to be born. Do not stop Breaking Through now.

What is stopping you is not what is stopping you. It is only deceiving you into believing that you can be stopped. You are unstoppable. You can only be deceived into believing that you will not succeed.

It is time to break through the deception and no longer allow the lies to occupy space in your mind.

It is time for me to break free!

I used to think it was impossible to break 5 boards with my head, now I do it all the time. This is a metaphor of what you can accomplish, you can do things you may think are impossible once you develop a Break Through mentality.

PART II:

THE FORMULA

One of the best ways to illustrate a breakthrough is the launch of a rocket ship. Imagine as it takes off that rocket ship is carrying almost a million pounds of fuel. It uses all kinds of energy, and yet, it takes off very slowly. If a rocket ship were human, it would be frustrated with itself for putting out so much energy with very little or slow progress.

It takes off very slowly, and then starts to gain momentum and speed. Right before it hits what we call "escape velocity," that rocket ship begins to rotate wildly, almost as if it's about to be broken into pieces.

Can you identify with this situation? Perhaps your relationship feels like it is about to be broken into pieces, you need a breakthrough. Maybe your finances or business seems almost at the place of ruins, you need a breakthrough. Perhaps it is your emotional, spiritual or psychological life that is coming apart and you know you need a breakthrough. Whatever area of your life is broken or about to be, you are in a similar state to that rocket ship, you feel like you are about to be shaken to pieces, the bottom even may be falling out.

Let me tell you something: Do not back down. If you back down, you may break down. If you continue on, you can experience the breakthrough that you desire and deserve.

Let me finish with the illustration. Imagine that the rocket ship is rotating wildly. The next instant it breaks through what we call escape velocity. Now it is traveling 25,000 miles per hour and virtually uses no more fuel.

Ninety-five percent of the consumed fuel is from take-off to escape velocity. Once the ship breaks through the Earth's atmosphere, there's no more shaking, it's smooth sailing, and it virtually uses no more fuel for the rest of the trip! It is just short of miraculous and a phenomenon that is almost breath taking. Your break through is akin to the rocket ship, and it usually only happens after great turmoil.

You must understand the thought provoking principle, a breakthrough is both sudden and gradual. We all like the sudden part, but the break through actually started at the point of take off and gradual ascension.

What if the rocket ship turned back in the midst of the shaking before it escaped the pull of the earth's atmosphere? It would be like millions of people today who have never experienced their greatness, because they quit when things got rough, they threw in the towel because of their pain. They stopped just three feet from their personal goldmine.

Well my friend, you may be just one-step from a massive breakthrough. I am going to assist you to get the breakthrough that you desire and deserve. It has happened for me and it has happened for many others. Now, it is going to happen for you, if you apply my seven-step breakthrough formula.

A formula is something that works every time by everyone who works it. The key is this:

- Nothing works until you do.
- You have to implement it.

My friend, I am so glad that you are investing in yourself enough that you want a breakthrough. I want you to have a breakthrough in many areas of life. You are going to experience massive breakthroughs as you implement my seven-step breakthrough formula.

When I talk about a seven-step breakthrough formula, these are time tested proven steps that will ensure your success.

I want you to understand that my formula is a system. I love the power of "systems." The acronym for "systems" shows you the power of a system.

S	-	*Save*
Y	-	*Your*
S	-	*Self*
T	-	*Time*
E	-	*Energy*
M	-	*Money*
S	-	*Stress*

Do you know anyone who would like to save themselves time, energy, money and stress? Would you agree that most people are interested in saving themselves time, energy, money, and stress?

It is amazing the success I have enjoyed in different business ventures as an entrepreneur. Success is not a secret; it is the result of developing, and/or following a system. I teach people that if you can develop a system, then you can put the system to work for you.

Moreover, the same thing applies with my breakthrough formula. The exception is I have done the hard part and developed it. It has taken me 30 long years to formulate all the components together into their proper sequence. All you have to do is apply the principles once you familiarize yourself with them.

When you have this breakthrough formula/system, then the system will do the work if you just implement it as soon as possible. "Information without implementation leads to frustration." Does this make sense to you thus far? Good.

Let us continue because you may be just one or more step(s) from a massive breakthrough.

May I boldly proclaim, I guarantee if you do as I have written, you will experience one or more breakthroughs.

I have to caution you that as Dr. Break Through I cannot *provide* a break through; all I can do is *prescribe* a break through. Yet, when you believe and implement the prescription, God Almighty <u>will</u> provide the Break Through. Just as a doctor cannot heal you, your best chance of healing is in following the doctor's orders; yet, even then, healing may not take place.

A good doctor is really one who is an educator. They listen intently to the patient's woes, then they carefully prescribe what they believe will help, based on the information they received.

The very best scenario is when the doctor can educate the patient on what to do in order to stay healthy. The best patient is the one who wants to know how they can obtain optimum health. They want to stay healthy so they will not have to come back to see the doctor.

After listening to people's woes for many years, I developed this formula/system so they can experience their break through.

CHAPTER 1

FORGIVENESS

Your Break Through

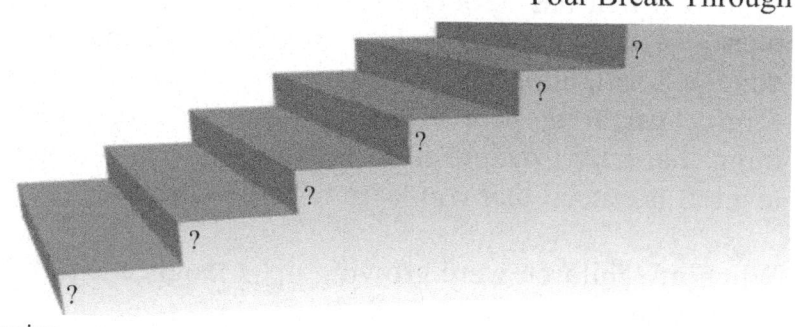

1. Forgive

The First Step Is **Forgiveness.**

If you want to have a breakthrough, you are going to have to learn to forgive. Usually, when we are in need of a breakthrough, we feel like that rocket ship that is about to break through escape velocity and is about to be shaken to pieces.

The need for a breakthrough usually denotes we are in a place of frustration, hurt or even desperation. It all seems to no avail because the awaited breakthrough has yet to arrive. We want to get through to the next level, but nothing we do seems to get us there. You have to learn and implement the first step of my formula, which is forgiveness.

I had to learn to forgive those teenagers who tarred and feathered me and beat me to a pulp. I had to learn to forgive my father for never coming around, for not sending money to mother and for not being there for me. I had to learn to forgive society. I had to learn to forgive my brothers.

I had to learn to forgive those who did not even show remorse for their wrongdoing.

You have to learn to forgive others, if you are going to experience your breakthrough.

Who is it that has wronged you and you have not forgiven them? Is it your mom, dad, ex-husband/wife, parents, son, daughter, neighbor, friend, employer, etc.? Not extending forgiveness holds people down. A lack of forgiveness is a thing that keeps people from breaking through to the next level. It is crucial that you learn to forgive others.

When my children were growing up, I taught them that life was not fair.

I would say, "Repeat it."

I would call each one of their names. I would start off with the oldest, "Christina, let me hear you say, 'Life is not fair.'"

She would say, "Life is not fair."

I would then repeat the same lesson with Joshua, Josiah, and then Justin.

Now, I am saying the same thing to you concerning how unfair life seems to be, especially when we need a break.

It is simple, yet true, "life is not fair."

I would then say to them, "Life is not fair, but God is fair (though at times it doesn't seem like it).

"One day, all the unfair things will be made right, but as long as you're in this life, you have to understand life is not fair."

You need to learn to forgive others. You need to learn to forgive life. You may even need to forgive God. When unexplainable things happen and we feel like, "God, why did you let this happen, why didn't you stop my abusers, why did you let my loved one die before their time (our estimation)?"

Sometimes bad things happen to good people for no apparent reason and we are tempted to wonder and ask God why? If you think God has done something that's not right, then you just need to forgive Him. Not that God needs your forgiveness (His ways are above our ways), but you need to do it because you need to have a breakthrough. You will never have a breakthrough unless you learn to practice the principle of extending forgiveness.

Sometimes you have to forgive yourself. I say this because you have tried things and you have failed. You tried again and you failed. We all let ourselves down and do not always perform as we would feel we could or should.

If you are like me, I am a "type A" driven personality. I have high goals, dreams and aspirations. I have times when I let myself down (how about you?). If you are not careful, you will get upset with yourself for under achieving. You have to learn to forgive yourself for not reaching your goals, dreams and/or aspirations.

You have to forgive yourself for the crazy mistake that you did or the down out wrong that you committed. For some people, the forgiveness of self is the greatest thing that they will ever learn. I know it was one of the hardest things for me to learn. I was always extra hard on myself. I am free to do better because I have balanced the hardness with forgiveness.

Why do I keep pressing the need to forgive yourself and others? A lack of forgiveness is negative energy that can hold you back. By the way, that negative energy is the thing that keeps you locked in the prison. The key that unlocks the prison doors is in your possession; it is the key of forgiveness. Please, use it now so you can go free!

Although heart disease has been identified as the #1 killer, doctors are finding out that anger, and bitterness are actually tied to the cause of heart malfunctioning. The root of anger can be traced to a lack of forgiveness.

Somebody said, "Bitterness does more harm to the vessel in which it is stored than the victim on whom it is poured."

When you have hate/anger within, the person you hurt the most is yourself. Drinking poison and looking for someone else to get sick is akin to anger, resentment and bitterness.

The old African proverb says it best, "If there's no enemy within, the enemy without, can do you no harm."

You have been hurt enough. Now is the time for you to experience your breakthrough.

There have been times when simply writing a letter has assisted me in experiencing a breakthrough in the area of forgiveness. You can write a letter explaining the pain you have endured. You can write a letter to the offending person explaining how badly they hurt you. Express all of your anger, disappointment, disillusionment, etc. Write a letter, then take the letter, fold it up and put it in an envelope, you can mail it, or you may choose to burn it. The activity of getting it off your chest is what is most important.

I advise you to do whatever is necessary to experience forgiveness. Major breakthroughs happen on this first step of forgiveness, major breakdowns occur with a lack of forgiveness. The choice is simple (not easy).

I will never forget the story of the older slave in the days of old. By the way, slavery was an unjust and wicked institution. This young slave said to the older slave, "Don't you just hate the master? I mean, he has control over our lives, and look at all the bad things he does." The old wise slave said, "No, I don't hate the master." The young slave said, "Aren't you a man?" The old wise man said, "Young man, I believe in being a man, but if I allow bitterness to rule my heart, I ain't a man no more."

That's bad English, but a powerful message!

I am thinking of the story of a young woman whose body was ravished by a wicked man who left her for dead. Someone found her, she was rushed to the hospital, and when she finally came to she was blind. Someone said to her, "Don't you just hate the man that did this to you? Don't you just hate him and wish you could hurt or kill him?"

She responded, "I never think about it." The person was shocked and said, "What do you mean?" She said, "He stole one night of my life. I refuse to give him one more minute."

Jesus said something very interesting, he said, "Father, forgive them, for they know not what they do."

This is a powerful lesson that has changed my life completely. You need to understand that people that do you wrong, do not always comprehend the extent of the pain they have inflicted upon you with their words, actions, and/or deeds. In other words, they may not be aware of the extent of the pain, but if you can learn to be aware of the fact that they are unaware of what you are going through, it helps to ease some of the pain. I call it being aware of the unawareness of others.

If you want to have a massive breakthrough, you have to ask others to forgive you. You cannot hurt people and continue your life as normal. Life will weigh down on you until you ask those whom you have wronged to forgive you. They may not forgive you, but your part is done once you ask.

When I do a live presentation, I often give those who want to, a chance to break a board. Occasionally, when people hit the board, it does not break. I am thankful that no one has ever hurt their hand in one of my breaking seminars. I, myself, have had times when I hit a board or stack of bricks and they didn't all break the first time.

Instead of getting angry and frustrated with myself, I have had to learn that the more frustrated I allow myself to get the more frustrated I become.
It throws off my energy and my focus until I stop and speak to myself. I say something like, "Stan, you're using your energy in a negative way and you're actually using your own energy against yourself." It has been called shooting yourself in the foot or friendly fire. Any term you give to this activity, you still understand it is not the best use of your energy.

Forgiveness is the first step, the part of this formula that perhaps will give you the massive breakthrough that you need right now. Maybe you need to forgive your father, your son or daughter, your husband or your wife. You need to forgive them, even if the person doesn't ask for it or deserve it, because you deserve to have your breakthrough! Perhaps the tears are flowing now, it' okay. Just say out loud, right now, _____ I forgive you.

I have broken through verbal, physical, sexual abuse, etc., and it all starts with forgiveness. Please, I beg you, do it now - you will be glad you did.

Picture the rocket ship that drops the extra boosters - so it can go higher. Picture the hot air balloon that has to drop some sand bags to go higher. Again, I ask you, for your health's sake, for the sake of your breakthrough - forgive (or ask to be forgiven). I am not saying that it is going to be easy, what I am saying is it is worth the effort.

Where I got tarred and feathered 43 years ago

About to Break Boards with Head

Line Up of Boards & Things to Break

CHAPTER 2

FAITH

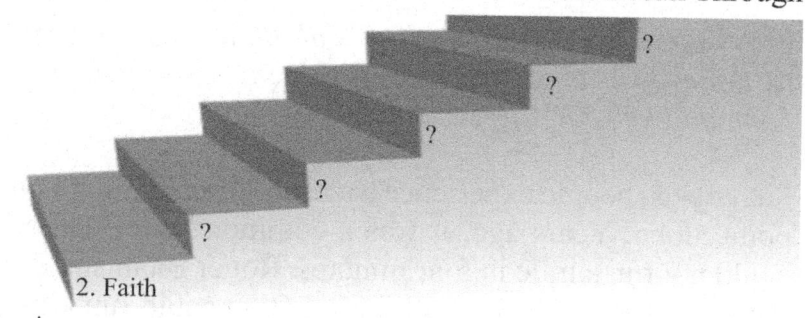

Your Break Through

2. Faith

1. Forgive

Step Two Is **Faith.**

"My reins (innermost being) also instruct me in the night seasons" Psalms 16:7.

There are times that if we would just get still, our heart would provide the insight needed to continue on. Some people get a face lift, but from time to time we all need a faith lift!

F	-	*Find*
A	-	*Answers*
I	-	*In*
T	-	*The*
H	-	*Heart*

Here is another acronym for "Faith."

F	-	*Forsaking*
A	-	*All*
I	-	*I*
T	-	*Trust*
H	-	*Him*

Prov. 3:5- *"Trust in the Lord with all thine heart and lean not to thine own understanding. In all thy ways acknowledge Him, and he shall direct…"*

I have seen people experience a massive breakthrough on this point alone. Years ago, it was a common belief that a man could not run a mile in four minutes. Roger Bannister did not embrace that belief. He had faith that he could run a mile in less than four minutes, and in 1954 on a nasty day at Oxford University, he ran it in only 3:59.4! Forty-six days later John Landy ran a mile in 3:58.

By the way, if you are ever going to have a breakthrough, you have to understand that, "most of the things in life worth doing, were declared impossible by someone else before they were accomplished."

Therefore, you have to have this breakthrough mentality. You have to use this second part of the formula called "Faith," which is just strong belief.

Henry Ford said, "There are only two kinds of people in the world, those who believe they can and those who believe they can't, and both are right."

"As a man thinketh in his heart, so is he" Proverb 23:7.

It takes faith, so allow me to refer to the illustration of breaking a board. You have to believe that you can break a board.

When I perform my martial arts demonstrations, I may stack up to 22 inches of cement blocks and then I break them with a hammer fist strike.

At times, I will lie on a bed of razor-sharp nails and put 100-pounds of cement blocks on my stomach, then a big man uses an 18-pound sledge hammer to swing and break the bricks off of my stomach, I then jump up and speak. People tend to listen to whatever I say next. (smile)

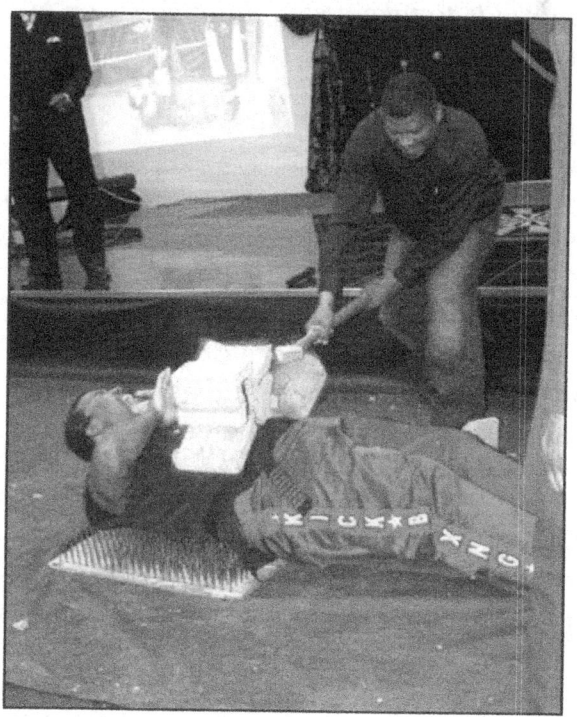

I then call about 10 strong men and women from the audience to the front of the room and let them punch, elbow, or kick me as hard as they can in the stomach.

Upon impact, I just stand and laugh as they bounce right off.

There was a time when I thought doing such things were impossible. I even take a steel bar and put it in my mouth; I then bend that steel bar. I used to think it was impossible to bend steel with your teeth. As long as I thought it was impossible to bend steel in my mouth, I never even tried.

That is why I am telling you that you have to have faith in whatever you want to accomplish regardless of how hard or difficult it seems.

> *Faith sees the victory, doubt sees the way.*
> *Doubt sees the dreary night, faith sees the day.*
> *Doubt dreads to take a step, faith soars on high.*
> *Doubt yells out, "Who believes?"*
> *And faith yells back, "I!"*
> *-Anonymous*

Mark 9:23, *"If thou canst believe, all things are possible to him that believeth."* (There is no gender, race or age barrier.)

Remember, people said they did not believe a man could run a mile in four minutes. They said it would be physically impossible and that the lungs would explode. Today, they tell me if a high school track runner cannot run a mile in 4 minutes, they are considered average.

You see, Roger Bannister had a breakthrough because he had faith and he believed. Your breakthrough is coming when you have faith and when you believe. It also will inspire others!

When folks asked Donald Trump, "To what do you attribute your success?" He said, "Well, I figured I had to think about something. And if I'm going to think, why not think big?" The bigger I thought, the bigger opportunities presented themselves to me, and I took big action and I got big results.

You have to believe something, so since you are going to believe in something, why not believe in faith? Some people say, "Fake it until you make it." I say FAITH it until you make it. You have to learn to trust and have faith.

I'm reminded of the old pitcher Satchel Paige, who pitched for the Negro Leagues years ago, when everything was separated and segregated.

Satchel Paige was such a powerful pitcher and had such faith and belief in his pitching ability that he would tell the outfielders, "Go ahead and sit down, because I can strike this guy out all by myself."

Can you imagine stepping up to bat and it is just you and the pitcher, no outfielders? They said Satchel Paige would tell the person at bat, "Get ready, because I'm about to strike you out." He would proceed to throw his famous curve ball.

The batter would swing, "Strike One!"

Satchel Paige would say, "You should just give up now and sit down before I embarrass you and strike you out with no one in the outfield."

He would throw a second pitch, the man at bat would swing and miss. The umpire would yell, "Strike Two!" and then the third pitch, "Strike Three!"

Satchel Paige would say, "I tried to tell you, didn't I? I tried to warn you."

When I read that story, I thought, "If a man could have that much faith, that much belief in his pitching ability, how much more faith should I have that I will experience my breakthroughs?"

The great people in life who have had breakthroughs are people who utilize faith. You have to believe that you can.

Believe That You Can

If you think you are beaten, you are.
If you think you dare not, you won't.
If you would like to win but think you can't,
It's almost a cinch you won't.

If you think you will lose, you've already lost.
For, this powerful truth we find,
Success begins with a person's will,
It's all a state of mind.

Life's battles don't always go
To the stronger woman or man,
But sooner or later those who win are those
Who first think, and then know that they can.
                                    - Anonymous

My breakthrough friend, I know you can!

I believe the reason you are reading this book now is that you had faith that you would one day experience a breakthrough. Deep inside your inner most being you have longed for a breakthrough.

As the old adage says, "When the student is ready the teacher will appear."

The most beautiful thing I love about faith is that even when we do not have faith in ourselves, we can connect with people who have faith, who see things in us that we do not see. We are too close to the forest to see our own trees.

Many of the things that I accomplished in my earlier years, I actually did not believe I could do them. I had people around me that I respected, that believed that I could, and I did not want to let those people down. I attempted to do things based on their belief in me, rather than my lack of belief in myself.

I was shocked; I accomplished things on their faith in me.

Just like when you learned to ride a bike, you used training wheels. Even if you do not have great faith in yourself at the present, I want you to know that I have faith in you! I believe in you! You can use my faith, like a young child uses training wheels, until your faith kicks in. You can accomplish some great breakthroughs on my faith, or the faith of those who believe in you!

I want you to understand, there are so many things that people accomplished by actually tapping into the belief of others. This is why coaches, trainers, and mentors are so important to your Break Through. Let me share with you a few things about what I have labeled "faith breakers" and "faith builders."

There are things that will build, and others that will break down your faith. If you understand these principles and you want your faith to be increased, simply avoid faith breakers and apply faith builders.

Listening to negative people will break down your faith. It would shock us if we knew how many times a person has listened to someone else's negative opinion and allowed it to diminish and even destroy their faith. Others' negative opinions of me are none of my business! I stay out of their business and let them keep it to themselves.

You have to guard yourself from spending excessive time with people who are pessimistic and negative, who use their tongue to try to cut you down. You even have to be careful of some family members. You may need to delete the phone numbers of a few people or send them to voice mail when they call. You must learn to guard your spirit from negativity.

The Most Dangerous People

The most dangerous people are not the ones
Who hit you with clubs and rob you with guns.
The thief won't attack your character traits
Nor belittle your abilities to your face.

It likely will be a well-meaning friend,
Who merely crushes your will to win.
No, he doesn't rob you at the point of a gun;
He simply says, "It can't be done."
When pointed to many who already are,
He smiles and says, "They're better than we are.
Personality-wise and abilities, too,
They're way ahead of what others can do."

And it matters not that his words are untrue
For you feel that others must know you.
So you're robbed of your hopes, your dreams to succeed,
Robbed of the faith that makes you believe,
And left to doubt if you'll ever achieve.

So the deadliest of people is not he with a gun,
But he or she who tells you, "It can't be done."
For, that taken by burglars can be gotten again,
But nothing can replace your will to win.
- Anonymous

I do not understand how people who say they want to succeed in life, spend a lot of time with people who do not care about their success. I learned early on in life to distance myself from those who drain my faith, and to engage myself with people who help build my faith.

Another thing that will break down your faith is doubt. All of us are human and we all have to deal with doubt. If you feed your doubt, it will starve your faith.

Two men talked about having faith and doubt. The younger one said, "I have faith but I also have doubt, this creates inner conflict. I need some help." The older man said, "Think of it this way, it's like you have two dogs.

"You have the dog of faith and the dog of doubt, and the determining factor of which one will be victorious is determined by the one you feed the most."

You want to starve out the doubt with faith, and so you need to participate in the activities that help build faith. Obviously, ways to build your faith would include spending time with people who are high energy, positive people.

I read that "Faith cometh by hearing." Your faith can be encouraged. Your faith can be uplifted and restored. Faith can be increased when you hear and read these powerful positive principles.

By the way, the reason I read biographies is that reading the biographies of successful people increases my faith.

Speaking is another way of building your faith. Here is a quote I love. I use it all the time. Muhammad Ali said, *"I said I was 'The Greatest' a long time before I ever believed it."*

I really like that statement! It is so powerful and needed today. Now read that again, aloud, and feel the surge in your faith.

Muhammad Ali started proclaiming that he was "The Greatest" even though he did not fully believe it; he had doubt about it. He said it long enough until other people believed it, and he said it long enough until he finally believed it. He will go down in history as one of, if not, "The Greatest."

You have to say what you want, even if you do not completely believe it. Why, because when you say things aloud you hear it, and as you hear it, you increase your faith.

Now that you are really serious and ready to experience your breakthrough, you must daringly proclaim your breakthrough as if it has already happened. You have to claim your victory now. You have to claim your breakthrough. The two most powerful words in the human language are the words "I am." Use them in the present tense. "I am breaking through to the success that I desire and I deserve."

How many of you remember Murphy's Law? You know Murphy's Law: "Anything bad that can happen will happen, and it will happen at the worst possible time."

Years ago, things were going so badly that it seemed like Murphy had moved in with me.

I got upset about it and I had to kick him out. First, I did not like Murphy's Law, and I sure did not like the results of his law, do you?

I developed my own law and I call it "Dr. Break Through's Law." It reads as such:

My Break Through Law

Anything good that can happen will happen, and it will happen at the best possible time.

Wow! I like that. I mean, I really like my law. In fact, it has changed my life and countless others. Now, it is your turn to say it out aloud! Say it every day for 30 consecutive days and you will receive tremendous value.

In summary, if you are going to have a breakthrough, you must have powerful faith, and you must learn to say some powerful things that will increase your faith. If your faith is not powerful, you must tap into another's faith until your faith becomes strong enough to stand on its own.

Now it is time to break free from the lack of faith that has kept you bound!

My Break Through Motto:

"Around me are bountiful opportunities.
Before me are endless possibilities.

Within me is the one who has infinite power,
And behind me, who cares?

I'm succeeding in a great way,
And it's getting better day by day.

Watch out world, here I come!"

We need to build our faith. We need to have our faith elevated. When you get to that place, your breakthrough is just around the corner.

I wrote something years ago that I read every day. I call it, **My Daily Attitude Adjuster.** It is kind of what my good friend Zig Ziglar says; (I have spoken for him many times).

Zig says, "Most people need a check-up from the neck up, they have stinkin' - thinking." He also said, "Many people are suffering from hardening of the attitudes."

I often give people this quote, some short but powerful words that I heard years ago, "It's your attitude, not your aptitude that determines your altitude."

A good attitude is one of the greatest assets a person can have: it is a seemingly little thing, that makes a big difference. A physically attractive person with a bad attitude will be viewed as unattractive, while an unattractive person with a good attitude will be viewed as attractive.

Attitude and faith are closely connected. I read **My Daily Attitude Adjuster** to ensure that I am in the proper frame of mind, which also increases my faith. Negative people have little faith, while people with good attitudes have great faith.

I want to include what Devin Dixon recently said about my Attitude Adjuster before I spoke for his group.

Dear Dr. Stan "Break Through" Harris

I have been a motivator, leader, professional athlete, coach, many things and when you shared your Daily Attitude Adjuster with me I was amazed. It got me so fired up I asked your permission to use it on our Radio Show, which you so graciously granted. Since then we always start our show with the Daily Attitude Adjuster. We not only get tremendous value from reading it, we have countless listeners who say it has "changed their life."

At Ultimate Mind University we believe every human being should start and end their day with the Daily Attitude Adjuster. The Ultimate Mind University will do its part in sharing it with the world. Thank you Dr. Break Through you change people's lives for the better; you are truly one of a kind.

Devin Duane Dixon
Ultimate Mind University
Ultimate Mind Radio Show

My Daily Attitude Adjuster

Wow! What a great day to be alive. I feel dynamite! I like me. I accept me. I love me.

I am going to have a super fantastic day today, because I am too blessed to be depressed. I am too blessed to be stressed; too glad to be sad, too anointed to be disappointed, and too elated to be agitated.

Circumstances are aligning themselves in my favor. I am healthy, physically fit, and intellectually equipped. I have wisdom far beyond my years.

I am an extraordinary person with incredible abilities, which I will use to add value to other people. Because, I know as I help others reach their dreams, I will automatically reach my own.

I anticipate meeting the person or group of people today who are willing to use their power, wealth, and influence to help me achieve my dreams. All day long people will go out of their way to bless me.

Today, I will add great value to someone's life. I will show compassion to those in need. I will give strength to the weak and inspiration to the weary. Someone needs what I have to offer and I gladly make myself available.

I embrace abundance and it embraces me. I am abundant in every good way. I am an abundance magnet. I like money and it likes me. It is attracted to me and comes abundantly from many sources. I use my money wisely, and help those in need.

I am experiencing great victories, supernatural turnarounds, and miraculous breakthroughs in the midst of great impossibilities. I am an overcomer. If my mountain can't be removed. I will develop and practice my mountain climbing skills.

I was broke, busted, and disgusted, but now I am rich, growing, and overflowing. I may experience a setback, but setbacks are only setups for comebacks. Setbacks pave the wave for comebacks.

I will make lemonade out of life's lemons, and if life dares to knock me down, I will fall on my back, realizing that as long as I can look up, I can get up.

I commit to paying for my dreams with preparation so that I won't have to live with my nightmares of regret. I do not procrastinate, because procrastination leads to devastation. It is the assassination of my destination. Thus, I will act now!

I am a doer! I get results that last.

I now release the champion that is inside of me. I am the leader that many people are looking for. I choose to succeed today and every day hereafter. Watch out world, here I come!

Send me an Email if you want a free mp3 set to music, DrBreakThrough@aol.com or DrBreakThrough@gmail.com, you can also get the hard copy.

Do you feel and sense the power of my Attitude Adjuster? All of those "I am" statements are empowering statements that I read to increase my faith, and they help me to conceive, believe, and achieve.

Booker T. Washington said, "Everything in life that I began to do, I began with the idea, I can and I will succeed."

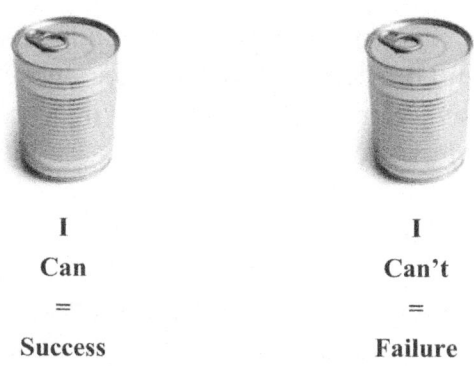

I	I
Can	**Can't**
=	**=**
Success	**Failure**

Success comes in cans but failure comes in can'ts.

By the way, instead of saying "I can't," eliminate the "T" from "can't," and now it reads, "I can." Do you sense your faith increasing?

Bill Gates sold what we now know as Microsoft on an idea that was not yet completed. He then decided not to create but rather buy it for $50,000. He even had to borrow the money. His partner wanted out after his faith dwindled. Bill now owns the whole company. Secretaries and janitors became millionaires. The rest is history.

Years ago, a young man, Jeffery Washington, was part of our Isshin'ryu Karate class. One person would sit on top of another person's shoulders and hold a board about 9 feet in the air, Jeff would jump up, kick and break the board. I was always so fascinated with his ability to accomplish such a task.

Each of us had our own part to perform during the demonstration. I would watch with amazement as he did his part. I often wondered how in the world someone could jump that high and kick a board. By the way, this is a vertical leap; no running and jumping, just jump and kick the board.

One day, Jeff had an emergency and consequently he was unable to attend the demonstration. In Japanese, you call your teacher "Sensei." Sensei means teacher/instructor. My Sensei said to me, "Harris, come here."

I replied, "Yes sir!"

"Jeff had an emergency and could not attend, I want you to take his place. I want you to jump up and kick that board."

My first thought was, "Sensei is crazy, I can't jump that high." However, my second thought was, "He believes I can do it, he is the instructor and leader. I don't know why he picked me; maybe he knows something I don't know."

I thought, "Well, if Sensei thinks I can do it, perhaps I can." In my mind, I remember watching Jeff kick. I played it back several times in my mind's eye. I bent down, jumped and kicked with everything in me. I actually had my eyes closed. To my utter surprise, I heard the board break. People started clapping as I landed on my feet.

I was shocked. I said to myself, "I did it! I did it."

I did it based on my Sensei's belief and/or command.

Faith is so strong. Even if it is someone's faith in us, it still can help us accomplish great breakthroughs.

In the many years that I have traveled both nationally and internationally, I do not jump quite as high now as I used to jump. I show people a picture in my wallet of me jumping 9 1/2 feet in the air kicking a board. Over 10,000 people attended years ago at the Hammond Civic Center in Hammond, Indiana.

People look at my picture in shock and amazement and ask this question, "How did you ever learn to jump that high, how long did it take you to learn how to do that?"

I say, "I never really learned. I just had faith. I took action on someone's faith in me, I tried it and it happened. The best part was that it was immediate, almost instantaneous."

You have to believe as I tell you this, and you have to release the champion that is on the inside of you. I love speaking to young people and informing them that the mark of greatness is upon them and that they have a champion in them. It is time to release the champion, let your inner winner come out.

Recently, my good friend Les Brown and I were in London, England speaking. I was supposed to close out the seminar. The seminar was scheduled to be over at 6 p.m.

I was supposed to speak from 5:15 to 6 p.m. Les was supposed to be done at 5p.m. but he went 60 minutes over his time until 6 p.m. Unfortunately, the audience thought the seminar was over, so they began leaving.

The seminar promoter was so embarrassed. I told him not to worry, but rather quickly introduce me. I jumped up and started speaking.

People were leaving because they thought the seminar was over. I said to myself, "I'm not going to let this happen. I'm going to bring these people back in."

I spoke with such fervor. People stopped in their tracks, turned and walked back inside to hear me speak. When I finished, the promoter said to me:

"I can't believe this! After Les Brown finished speaking, I thought, 'What else could anyone speak on?' Then he went over time and everybody was leaving, and I just thought, 'What else could happen?'

"It was amazing how you started speaking and people started coming back in. And some people had such a life transformation breakthrough from hearing you."

I asked him, "Do you know why that happened?" He answered, "No, but I would really like to know." I replied, "Because I had faith, because I really believe the message someone needs to hear the most can only be received when they hear me."

Believe me when I tell you on this one point alone, people have experienced great breakthroughs.

At some of my seminars, I have people come forward who desire to break a board.

I tell them, "First of all, I would not have you try to break this board unless I absolutely, positively knew you could break a board.

Now, you just need to believe it and break the board."

My book called, Mental Self Defense: Learning How to Defend Yourself Against Your Greatest Opponent, which is your undisciplined or subconscious mind, will help your thought process.

Are you ready to take the next step that will get you closer to your breakthrough?

Read on because the next step is very thought provoking.

**Helping
8 Year Old
Break Board**

**Even an
8-year-old
boy can break
a board!**

CHAPTER 3

FACTS

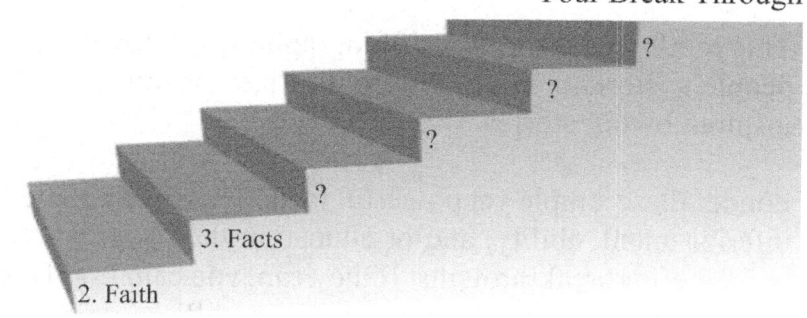

Your Break Through

?
?
?
?

3. Facts

2. Faith

1. Forgive

Step Three Is **Facts.**

The third step of my powerful breakthrough formula is simply the word "facts." If you are going to have a breakthrough, you have to extend forgiveness, you have to have faith, but then you have to know some empowering facts.

Proper facts fuel your faith. It is inspiration without instruction that leads to frustration. There are some empowering facts that I will cover that will help fuel your faith.

By the way, I want you to know that if you are a healthy person, 12 years of age or older, you can break a board.

Fact: The bone in your hand is 80 times harder than a pine board.

When I learned that fact, it fueled my faith. In fact, I was afraid to break a board until I saw my Mom...

When I saw my Mom break a board without any injuries, I said, "Wait a minute! If my Mom could break a board, I can break a board." Guess what? I did break a board.

This reinforces the power of biographies, the power of other people's stories. They inspire us, just as others will be inspired by our stories.

Ponder these simple yet powerful facts. There are people with inferior talent, ability, and/or education than you, who have had superior breakthroughs. If they can, you can. I said if they did, you could. I said, if they have, you will!

"If others can and have broken through, we can as well. Someone is going to have a breakthrough, it might as well be me, and it might as well be you." If you understand these facts, it will fuel your faith.

This is why reading is so important and powerful. The man or woman who does not read is not a great deal better than the man or woman who cannot read (they are actually worse!). Therefore, you should applaud yourself for reading this book.

All four of my children have broken boards, and I have had seminars where an 8-year-old boy, all the way to an 86-year-old man has broken a board. They watched my breakthrough presentation, and decided to do it with my supervision and coaching.

I will never forget speaking in Dallas, Texas for a particular company, and a young lady stood up and said, "I want to break a board." At this particular demonstration, I had 110 boards for the 110 participants. I wanted them to experience a breakthrough by metaphorically breaking through a board that would show them that they could break through any barrier that stands in their way.

When I first called for people to come break the boards, I will never forget one woman stood up and said, "I want to do it."

I looked out and she was not young. Actually, she was 81 years of age. I responded, "Oh no, no, ma'am." I was thinking she might break a bone; she might have osteoporosis, or something. I saw a potential lawsuit.

However, you know when a woman has her mind made up, you might as well get out of her way. She said to me, "young man. I heard you speak, and I've been watching you. I believe I can do this."

I called her to the front of the room. I said to myself, "If she believes she can break a board, I better join in on her belief."

The woman came up and I had the crowd chant, "It's breakthrough time, breakthrough time, breakthrough time." Immediately this woman took her fist and broke through a 1-inch pine board to the shock and amazement of the crowd, as well as myself, without any bruises or pain. She did it!

When she broke her board, everyone in the room jumped up and said, "I want to break through now!"

Understand another powerful fact. When we have the opportunity to watch someone else experience a breakthrough, we are inspired to have our own breakthrough.

The fact is, if an 81-year-old woman can experience a breakthrough, you can experience a breakthrough.

When I was speaking a few months later in Philadelphia, Pennsylvania and I told that story, after I finished with my breakthrough demonstration, I had a few boards for those who wanted to attempt to have a breakthrough. One man jumped up (86 years of age) and said, "If an 81-year-old woman can do it, I can do it."

I replied, "No sir, please do not attempt to break a board, I won't be held liable, besides there are different ways to have a breakthrough."

He said, "No, no. I'm going to do this." And an 86-year-old man broke the board without any incident or injury.

DISCLAIMER:

Please Do Not Try This Without Some Assistance Or Training. What I Am Saying Is For Illustration Purposes Only.

Dr. Stan "Break Through" Harris

Years and years ago after seeing me do many demonstrations, my oldest son Joshua, not quite 5 years old at the time, was telling me how powerful I was and how proud he was to have me as his dad. I said to him, "Son, you come from me and your mother, you are powerful, and you can break a board."

He replied, "No sir, I can't break a board. Please don't make me."

I said, "Son, first of all, don't say, no you can't; say you *can*. Joshua, you can break this board. Let me hear you say, 'I can break the board.'"

He very sheepishly said in the question mark form, "I can break the board?"

I said, "No, no, son. Say it like you mean it. Say it with passion. Say it with determination and say, 'I CAN AND I WILL BREAK THIS BOARD.'"

He said it a little stronger, "I can and I will break this board."

I said, "Now say it again stronger and louder."

He said, "I can and I will break this board."

I had him say it repeatedly, finally I said, "Come on, son, hit it." He hit that board, it broke and I was shocked myself.

By the way, his sister Christina, who was a year older, said, "Daddy, I want to break the board. If Joshua did it, I can do it. Please Daddy, I am the oldest." I said, "You better not tell your mom." She promised not to tell, and then my little 6½ year old daughter proceeded to break the board.

I am telling you, these are powerful stories that are facts. When you understand the facts, it will increase your faith and assist you in breaking any barrier that tries to hinder you.

Here are the facts. In any area that you desire to have a breakthrough, there is someone who has had a breakthrough in that or a similar area.

The actions of a young woman extremely inspired me, when I was in Bowie, Maryland speaking for a seminar. I performed my breakthrough presentation. This woman heard me talk about my children, the 8-year-old boy, the 81-year-old woman, etc. This woman jumped up and said, "Although I have never broken a board, I believe I can do it."

Oh, did I forget to tell you? This woman did not have arms. She just had little stubs that did not quite come down even to her elbow level.

I thought, "Oh, my goodness, what have I done? I have inspired this woman so much she wants to try to break a board without arms. It's going to ruin my illustration, and perhaps conclude with her sustaining an injury."

I had to catch myself. "Wait a minute, I'm operating in doubt and I need to operate in faith. She believes she can do it, so I ought to support her belief." She came forward, jumped up, and broke that board with her little stub. Do I need to tell you that she jumped and screamed with excitement and exuberance, and people in the room started jumping and screaming?

Of course, the rest of the people in the room ran forward to experience breaking a board. We were all so inspired by this young woman who did not refer to her condition as handicapped, but rather handi-capable.

It is a very powerful fact; there are people that do not have all the things we have, yet have experienced great break-throughs.

I say, "If they can, we can. If they can, you can."

You are genetically encoded to experience breakthroughs. It is part of your very DNA.

Your first Break Through was when you had to beat over 40 million sperm cells to the womb and break through the walls. Yes, you beat them all, you came in first place, therefore, you are championship material. Perhaps you are just realizing this for the first time.

Your second Break Through was your actual birth, when the water broke, and you broke through the birth canal. Yes, you are a Break Through Master.

Now, go do what you were designed to do, that is Break Through. This is part of your birthright, breaking through is your destiny!

Another fact to breaking a board is that boards only break with the grain (lines) not against the grain (I learned this the hard way many years ago).

The middle of the board has less resistance than any part of the board, so that is the place to aim for maximum results.

FACTS

- You may be just one idea away from a million dollars.

- The greatest breakthrough has yet to be experienced.

- The greatest business has never been built as of yet.

- The greatest marriage has yet to be experienced.

- The great things in life are still awaiting your arrival.

- The greatest walk with God has yet to be experienced.

- You can do some powerful things that, perhaps to this point, you thought were impossible. Those things are not impossible. You just have not experienced them at this time, but keep striving because your time is near.

Now you know some facts that should make you hungry to learn even more empowering facts that will build your faith.

My friend, the chances are, you can accomplish what you desire if you will just ask or extend forgiveness, if you will have faith, and then become aware of powerful facts.

It is time to break free from the lack of knowledge that had you bound!

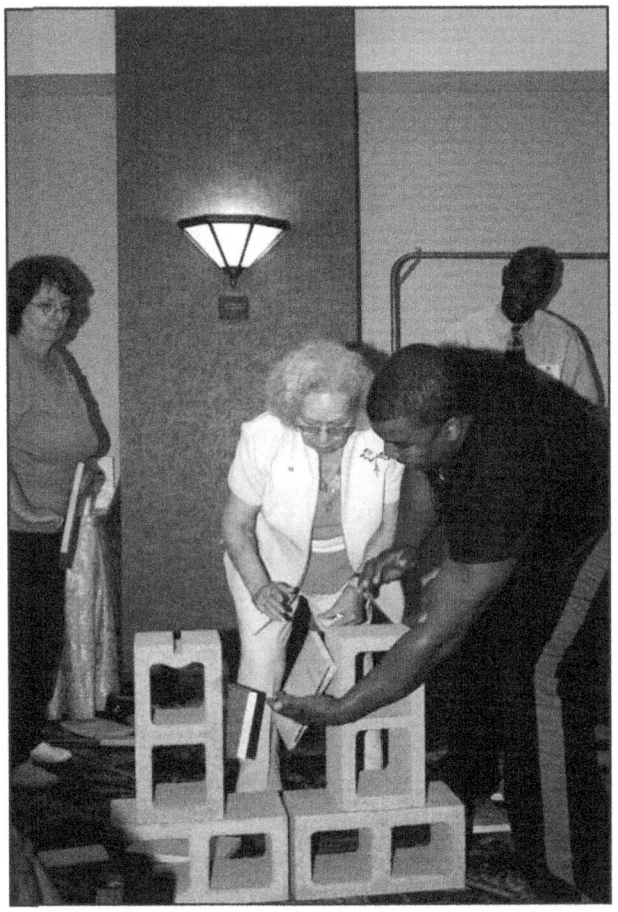

An 81 year old woman breaks a board!

CHAPTER 4

FOCUS

Your Break Through

?

?

?

4. Focus

3. Facts

2. Faith

1. Forgive

Step Four Is **Focus.**

The fourth part of this breakthrough formula/system is focus.

As a child, do you remember getting a magnifying glass and holding it over leaves?

As the rays of the sun went through the magnifying glass, it actually caused the leaves to catch fire and burn.

Are you aware that you can concentrate the rays of the Sun even more and create a laser that can cut through steel?

The power of focus is incredible. Slow down, learn to focus your power, and do not scatter it.

A wise man once said to me, "Young man, sometimes you have to slow down so you can speed up."

My acronym for focus is powerful:

F	-	*Firmly*
O	-	*On*
C	-	*Course*
U	-	*Until*
S	-	*Successful*

If you are going to experience your breakthrough, it is imperative that you practice the power of focus. One reason people never have the breakthrough they desire, is because they focus too much on what they want to break through.

Yes, I said many people never have a breakthrough because they are trying to break through. Understand this principle. What you focus on the longest becomes the strongest. When we need a breakthrough, it is something negative that we are trying to get through. Many people never have a breakthrough, because they are focusing on that negative thing. For instance, many people say they want to be debt free, so they focus on debt. Can you figure out why they end up in more debt, though they declare just the opposite? What you focus on the longest becomes the strongest.

You do not have a breakthrough by focusing on what you want to break through. You experience breakthrough when you focus on what you are committed to breaking to.

I have contemplated changing my branding from "Dr. Break Through" to "Dr. Break To." I teach, "If you focus on what you desire to break to, you will automatically break through where you are."

When breaking boards a person may write Fear on the front and Greater Success on the back. I instruct the person to aim (Break To) Greater Success (back of the board) and they will automatically Break Through Fear (front of the board). A person may have Procrastination on the front and Accomplishing More Tasks on the back, or Excuses on the front and Making Progress on the back. Can you see the power of focusing and aiming for what you want, thus automatically going thru what you do not want?

In other words, once you break to something you have automatically broken through something. The Breakthrough was a by-product, not the focus.

During this economic crunch, individuals and companies who focus on what they want to break to, will thrive, while those trying to break through the economic crunch will only get more turmoil and financial problems. This is why it is so imperative to practice concentration, imagination, and meditation/ visualization.

Let us revisit the example of breaking a board. I never attempt to break a board/stack of bricks, bend steel, or lay on the bed of nails, unless I have first accomplished it in my mind. If I cannot break the board in my mind, I will not try to break it physically. Imagination is so powerful. For this reason, the subconscious mind cannot differentiate between that, which is real, from that which is vividly imagined.

Did you ever have a bad dream that you were either, falling off a roof, being hit by a car or some other tragedy? Did you wake up scared or in a cold sweat? Really, what happened was simple. The mind was convinced of the reality of the situation, thus it discharged the energy to the body to respond accordingly.

I remember reading a book that talked about two different basketball teams that played each other. One team literally practiced in their mind, while the other team practiced on the court. When the two teams played together, the teams were equal. In some cases, the team that played in their mind beat the team that practiced every day. I am sure you are wondering why this was possible.

It was possible because the team that played in their mind visualized every shot as successful. In their mind, they saw themselves stealing the ball from their opponents. They saw themselves blocking their opponents' shots. They saw themselves perfectly dribbling down the court, without committing any fouls. They saw themselves shooting. They saw themselves winning, and that is exactly what happened.

If you can see it, you can be it, however, if you cannot see it, you will not...

Literally, the brain discharged the energy to the body to accomplish what it had seen.

How many times is a building constructed?

A) Once

B) Twice

C) Three times

To the man/woman who desired to build, it was constructed first in their mind. The second time it was constructed was on paper (blue prints), and the third time was when it was manifested where the rest of the world could see.

The same is true with your life. The same is true with you having a breakthrough. You can visualize yourself breaking through, and not just breaking through, but breaking to the success that you desire and deserve.

I first thought about entitling this book *Breaking Through Every Barrier That Hinders You*. Then, I realized it would have a negative connotation.

The more we focus on breaking through barriers and hindrances, the stronger they become.

However, if the title would become, *Your Break Through Is Guaranteed,* now we get people to focus on what they want in life and how they can get it through my seven step system. Any way that you describe or envision success is fine. I just want you to have that experience of your definition of success as soon as possible. Sooner is better than later in this case.

Here is a quote that will be featured in my next book, *Quotes That Can Make You Rich*. "You have to visualize vividly and verbalize veraciously (with passion) so you can soon actualize automatically."

In other words, what you visualize and what you verbalize, you will eventually actualize. I understand that some people say that affirmations do not work, but those are affirmations said without passion. When you are passionate about it and you visualize it, and then you verbalize it, you will actualize it.

When I say, "Visualize vividly," I mean to the point where you can almost see it, you almost hear it, you can almost reach out and touch/taste it. Close your eyes for a minute and imagine a tall cold glass of lemonade on a hot day in July.

I remember hearing a recording of my good friend Jim Rohn. He and I have spoken many times together. Jim, my mentor Bill Bailey and I were all speaking in Montana. I overheard Bill and Jim talking about the good old days.

Jim talked about the fact that he was in his imaginary house, and he said he described it so well to his friend, that his friend bumped his elbow on his imaginary fireplace. He said the day came when that imaginary house was a real house.

My breakthrough friend, just learn to focus on what you want because you only waste your time when you think about what you do not want.

There is a powerful book and documentary called The Secret. I like to say it is not a secret; it is scripture. Proverbs 23:7, *"As a man thinketh in his heart, so is he."* The whole film is based solely upon the fact that powerful people have understood, and practiced this principle; focus on your goals, not daily life.

They do not allow their mind to think about what happens to them and what is going on around them, but rather they focus their attention, focus their awareness and concentrate their thoughts on what they want to accomplish.

You have to discipline your mind to focus on what you want, instead of what seems to go on around you. At that moment, you start attracting your desires. If you want to break through to your success, it is imperative that you get what some people call a "Vision Board." I call it a *"Break To Board."*

Get a picture of the house you would like to live in, the car you would like to drive, the lifestyle you would like to live, the family, the happiness, etc.

Get pictures of all of these things and put them on your break to board. Focus your attention on them daily, the mind will discharge the energy needed to materialize, to bring to pass the things you seek.

When breaking boards, I talk about focus. If I use my fist, I use the first two knuckles and concentrate all of the power from the body and hand into those first two knuckles, just like a hammer. A hammer is so strong. It takes all of a person's energy and focuses it to a small area, the size of a dime, and because of that, it can break through things.

It is the same with the breaking of boards, whether I use the knuckles or what we call the hammer fist strike, which is the bottom part of the hand. The key is to use a small concentrated part of the hand, foot, elbow, or head.

During this time, I never allow my thoughts to say, "I wonder if they will break this time." I simply focus on seeing them broken, and then I make happen what I have already seen.

I recall a powerful story of a young Olympian who won the event and set a new record. As soon as she finished her particular swimming event, she put on a hat with the exact time that she had won the race.

A reporter asked, "How did you know that you would win in that time, to the point you had a hat done before the race"? She explained that in her mind she saw herself winning in that particular time.

She rehearsed constantly, and consistently.

Good thoughts and actions can never produce bad results! You must cultivate and guard powerful thoughts about what you want to accomplish.

My friend Artemis desperately wanted to get in shape. She had a friend who sent her a picture of a shapely woman that resembled Artemis in the face. Artemis placed a picture of her face over the model's face. In essence, it was a picture of how she wanted to look. It was not long until she started working out due to the inspiration of daily looking at the picture. Months later, Artemis got her picture taken, and to her complete surprise, her body mirrored the model's body. I actually saw both pictures and it is hard to tell them apart. Please understand things like this can happen for you as well.

That is why it is so imperative to be careful about what you watch on TV or the Internet, especially if you have young people. Their minds are constantly exposed and bombarded with terror and bad things. Do not underestimate the power of imagery. People wear, talk and even act out what they see.

You have to learn to turn off the amusement and focus on what you want, even though it may presently seem to be the furthest thing from your life.

I shall never forget, years ago, when I started a business and made almost $30,000 in my first month! Five months later, I earned over $100,000 for the month.

Up to that point, I had never made that much money in a whole year, let alone a single month!

What you really need to know, (I have never shared this story before with anyone), is that I was homeless when I started my business. I had never even been close to hard times like this previously.

Actually, I was staying with a friend. Through a business deal "gone bad," I also had lost my brand new car, even my cell phone, and was about to give up on my dignity. Someone actually paid my way into that opportunity.

You have to learn to focus on what you want, and then give attention to that. What you think about the longest becomes the strongest. What you talk about the longest becomes the strongest.

What you focus on the longest becomes the strongest. If you focus on your debt, you get more debt. If you focus on being financially free, you will be financially free.

Why waste focus on the poverty you may be experiencing, (you will just get more of it), concentrate instead on the prosperity you would like to experience.

Why focus on the problems of a relationship, (you will just get more of them), concentrate instead on imagining a peaceful relationship with the same person. Hold your focus long enough and it will happen, it will materialize.

May I share another life changing thought? *It is not what you do not have, but rather what you think you need that keeps you from breaking through to the success and/or happiness that you desire and deserve.*

When we focus on what we think we need to succeed, whether it's more education, another's help, money, ability, etc. we are focusing on what we do not have; thus we are coming from a place of lack/weakness.

Think and meditate on this powerful thought provoking thought again:

It is not what you do not have, but rather what you think you need that keeps you from breaking through to the success and/or happiness that you desire and deserve.

For instance, consider Bill Gates. He dropped out of college, and yet, there came a time when he was the richest man in the world. When you focus on what you think you need, you take your attention off what you already possess.

My good friend, Tawana Williams, wrote a book called *Unarmed But Dangerous*. She was born without arms, and yet today she is a powerful speaker, singer, wife, mother, artist, and author. She types faster with her feet than many people type with their hands.

She learned to change her baby's diaper with her feet, and braid the baby's hair with her feet. She also uses her feet to draw. She uses her voice to speak and sing.

When you hear/watch her sing the song, *"I Won't Complain,"* you say to yourself, "I'll never complain about anything again."

Too many people allow what they do not have to keep them from utilizing what they already posses. What about you?

I'm saying you need to focus on learning to use what you have, focus on where you want to go, focus on what you want to do.

Don't focus on what's happened in the past. Learn from the past and let the past be just that, the past.

Successful people have developed the skill to divert their attention from what could be called failures to what will be called successes.

Focus on how you will feel when you have that breakthrough.

Focus on how you would "feel" when you reach that place, have that car, marry that person, and/or have that thriving business.

Focus on that, and only that, time after time, after time!

This will assist you in breaking through to your success.

Close your eyes, see yourself driving the car of your dreams, living the life of your dreams, making the amount of $$$ you desire. Imagine having the freedom you want. Focus! Focus!

Take a minute and write a paragraph on how you would feel, if you were at this very moment at your desired place in life.

_____

_____

_____

_____

_____

_____

Where and when you focus is important. You cannot focus while in a very noisy area or while a houseful of children are playing. Find a quiet, secluded area. You may even need to wake up before everyone else. Break Through distractions to focus so that you can experience your Break Through!

Wow, you have made awesome progress! I congratulate you. If you have not had several breakthroughs or at least one breakthrough by now, you are about to learn and take the fifth step that will definitely bring you closer.

This motor home is on my break to board, I'll be riding in style!

Break Through to Your Wealthy Place

A picture is worth a thousand words . . .

and some words are worth a thousand pictures.
By Joshua Harris

"I love my wife!"

CHAPTER 5

FORCE

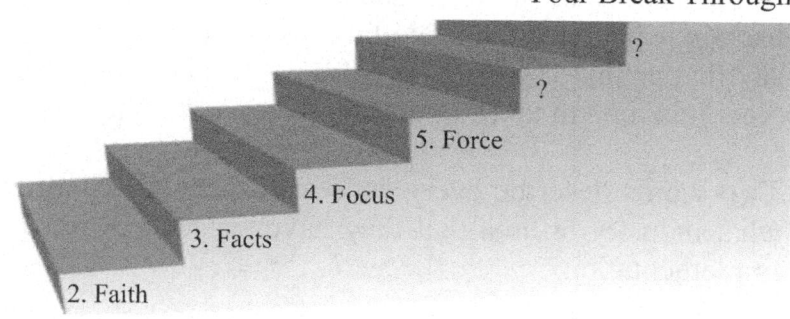

Your Break Through

Step Five Is **Force.**

The fifth step to the breakthrough system is what I call "force." Let me return to the illustration of breaking boards.

Some that have come to my seminars have said, "You know, I've tried to break a board before but it did not work." Even one person said he broke his hand in the Karate class he was in, and I replied:

"Well, I am going to show you how to do this almost effortlessly."

First, you have to forgive yourself for not being able to break the board. Secondly, you have to have faith and believe that you can. Even if your faith is weak, you need to believe the fact that I believe that you can. Thirdly, realize the fact that the bone in your hand is 80 times harder than wood.

Focus your attention and see the board breaking in your mind. See yourself hitting it. See the board break. See yourself jump up in jubilee and exuberance. Focus your attention on that. Then it is time to apply the force. It is now time to hit it.

I know folks who sit around all day, every day, meditating and concentrating on what they want, but without the step of taking action, of applying some force, nothing is going to happen. Understand this: Nothing works until you do. Let me say that again, "Nothing (not-a-thing) works until you do." Now it is time to take action, immediate action to be exact.

Two words describe every successful person, regardless of what industry or area that they have succeeded: Immediate Implementation.

The thing that helped me rise to the top in the Martial Arts, Business, as well as in life was the fact that I immediately implemented the things I learned. If you do not implement what you learn (even now in this book), you might start talking yourself out of doing them altogether.

MIT did a study and found that 83% of self-talk is negative. If you do not learn to take action immediately, you are going to talk yourself out of things. They also found it takes 17 positive comments just to offset one negative comment, and the 18th will bring you back to where you were. It is amazing, that you must hear 18 positive compliments to offset just one negative criticism.

At times, we are great critics of ourselves. In spite of any shortcomings, you have to learn to take action. Actually, you must take immediate, massive action, to implement the things that you have learned.

I give the illustration about five sparrows that were sitting on a tree limb, three decided to fly away, how many birds were left? Among the audience, people often reason to themselves, if you have five birds, and three decide to fly away, you have two left. Thus, they give "two" as their answer. I say, "Wrong," understand three *decided* to fly away, <u>but they never did anything about their decision.</u> *"It's the start that stops most people, don't let the start stop you."* Learn to take immediate massive action!

Here is a powerful quote that I developed: "When I make up my mind to do something, circumstances align themselves in my favor. When I say, 'I can't,' my mind stops trying. But, when I ask, 'How can I?' my mind keeps searching until it finds a way. There is a way, and I will find it, and if not, I will invent it." Remember, "Necessity is the Mother of Invention."

My friend, you have to understand something. As great as this formula is and as proven as it is, it will not work for you unless you learn to take this fifth step. You have to take action, and not just action, take immediate massive action.

You can be a very powerful person, even though you may not know a whole lot. If you do a whole lot, then you will experience some great breakthroughs. I want to encourage you to take action, apply force, and get going now!

In the Martial Arts, I tell people right before they hit the board that I want them to yell. We call that yell a ki-ya. Scientists have proven that you can increase your strength capacity by 10% just by yelling.

Have you ever noticed that some tennis players grunt when they hit the ball? Many boxers, arm wrestlers, and other athletes notice an increase in strength, just by exhaling heavily or yelling. I coach people who desire to break a board to yell just before impact. I also instruct them to think about something that gets them upset, and then transfer their aggression to the board.

If you are one-step from a massive breakthrough, that step is simply force, or using "immediate implementation." Take massive action right now!

How many people already know what they need to do, but simply lack the initiative to make it happen? Think of one thing that you know would produce tremendous results if you simply implemented it. So what are you waiting for, the perfect time? It will never come. Perhaps you are waiting for more training. Well, your greatest learning tool from here on will be the result of taking action.

Many things will not be learned fully until you get busy and move on what you know (regardless of how little it may be). I learned to speak by speaking! I am perfecting my speaking by speaking more and using reflection. (How could I have done better, etc?)

This just might be the best chapter of this whole book. So let me ask you a very pointed question. What is it that you need to do right now, perhaps even before you finish this book? (Make a phone call, write a letter…)

Recently, while speaking along this topic, a man jumped up, and bolted out the door right in the middle of my talk. The whole room was shocked but as he left he said, "I can't take this anymore, he's right, there is something I have to take care of, I have waited long enough."

Need I tell you, he experienced a tremendous Break Through as well as others in the room, because they were motivated to take action by his drastic action?

You may need to stop reading this very minute and make a phone call, or go visit somebody or do what you already know needs to be done.

If you rationalize, (allowing your mind to find excuses for what your inner being knows is right) telling yourself that you will do it later; you will lose the fervor and momentum and perhaps never get it done.

I sense you saying to yourself, "It is not that big of a deal, or I have been okay not doing anything thus far, why can't I just do it after I finish the book?"

This is an early state of delusion, which may lead to denial. Here is my acronym for denial. (Can you tell I like figuring out and using acronyms?)

D - *Don't*
E - *Even*
N - *Know*
I - *I*
A - *Am*
L - *Lying*

People who are in denial lie to themselves and thus lie to others, it's time to stop the lies and Break Through to integrity. When you finally open your eyes to the big lie "I already know this" you will be amazed at your growth. If you say you know something but you are not doing it, you don't really know it. You must come to grips with the truth that you can mentally ascent or acknowledge a truth without really knowing the truth. You only know what you do and/or act upon. You see sometimes you have to hear things many times before it sinks down from your head to your heart and thus your life. That's why I made this book edu-taining and life transformational, meaning that it educates, and entertains while it transforms.

I teach a session on "How to get the most from a seminar, workshop, service, etc." One simple point is to "find one thing that you can implement immediately, instead of being overwhelmed in trying to remember or implement the lessons of the entire seminar."

What can (your ability), and will (your level of commitment) you do right now? What will you do tomorrow? What will you do when you finish reading this book?

Your Break Through depends on it and perhaps others' breakthrough depends on it as well!

Me and Justin at the Airport

CHAPTER 6

FOLLOW THROUGH

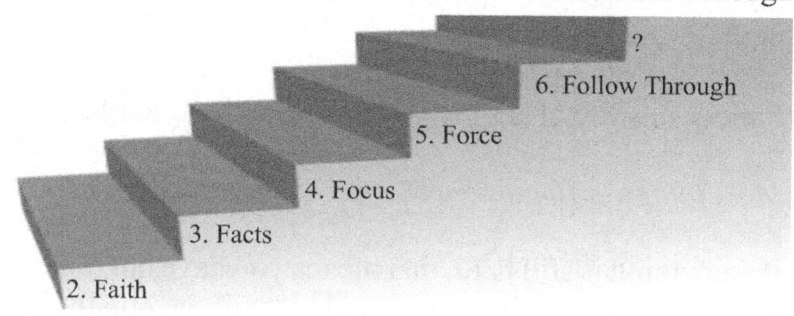

Your Break Through

?

6. Follow Through

5. Force

4. Focus

3. Facts

2. Faith

1. Forgive

Step Six Is Follow Through.

The sixth and next to the final step is follow-through. I return to my illustration of breaking a board.

I never aim at a board or at a stack of bricks. I always aim through them. I teach my students that if you are going to break a board, you need to aim about two to three inches below the board. Focus on and aim for the spot 3 inches past your object instead of just hitting the top of the board and stopping. If you are going to have a breakthrough, you have to follow through.

Many people start things but do not finish them. You have to employ the sixth step of my breakthrough system, which is follow-through.

Calvin Coolidge made a very powerful point when he said: "Nothing in the world can take the place of persistence. Talent will not. Nothing is more common than unsuccessful men with talent. Genius will not; unrewarded genius is almost a proverb. Education will not. The world is full of educated derelicts. Persistence and determination alone are almost omnipotent."

People, who follow through, are those who make up their mind, who make a commitment and say, "I'm going to do this until ..."

Ponder this life changing Break Through principle:

Most things in life are easy, after they are hard.

If something is still hard, that means you have not done it long enough. If you do it long enough, it will eventually become easy.

You have to make this Break Through commitment, *I am committed to the process of being bad for however long it takes to get good.*

When I started in Martial Arts 41 years ago, I was bad, but I was committed to the process. I stayed in long enough until they could get me good. When I started speaking years ago, I was bad, but I was committed to the process. I stayed in long enough until I got good.

When I began a home-based business, I was bad, yet I committed to stay in long enough so they could teach me how to be good. I could go on and on, like when I became a husband, father and coach. I was not very good, but I am now. Why? I lasted through the learning curve that causes the uncommitted to quit.

In this formula, you will Break Through, only after you follow through. The only time you find breakthrough before follow-through is in the dictionary.

When I hit a board or stack of bricks my only concern is stopping before I hit the ground. I have such a sold-out, committed and determined mind-set and so should you. When people make up their minds that they are going to have a breakthrough and that they are going to follow through, the breakthrough comes. Commitment to completion always produces champions.

Don't Quit
by Clinton Howell

When things go wrong, as they sometimes will,
When the road you are trudging seems all uphill.
When the funds are low and the debts are high,
And you want to smile, but you have to sigh.

If care is pressing you down a bit,
Rest if you must, but please don't quit.
Life is queer with its twists and turns,
As every one of us sometimes learns.

And many a person turns about,
When they might have won had they stuck it out.
Don't give up though the pace seems slow,
You may succeed with another blow.

Often the struggler has given up,
When they might have captured the victor's cup.
And they learned too late when the night came down,
How close they were to that golden crown.

Success is failure turned inside out,
The silver tint of the clouds of doubt.
You never can tell how close you are,
Victory may be near though it seems afar.
So stick to the fight when you're hardest hit,
It's when things seem worst that you must not quit.

Understand that a breakthrough is similar to getting the last number of a combination lock.

Do you remember those three number combination locks of years gone by? In some cases, it is like you have two of the numbers and you only need the third number. The lock almost comes open, but not quite. It is just one little piece, just one more number and all of a sudden it unlocks.

Whenever you start a new venture, it is easy to get excited. Enthusiasm prevails and passion persists. As time wears on, desire fails and passion fades. Remember the first time you got a brand new car (or even an older car that was new to you)? You constantly kept it clean both inside and out. Perhaps you parked away from other cars in parking lots to keep it from being scratched. After having it for a while, you say, "Oh well it's just a car."

Remember when you had or attended the delivery of your first child? You attended to every little thing; you took so many pictures. Then later, a second child arrived. Well, by the time the third or the fourth arrived, it's like, "Child, you're going to have to make it for yourself."

You literally prop a bottle up in the baby's mouth, and then hope everything will work out. (Okay, maybe I over exaggerated, a little.) If you or someone you know have several children, notice how few pictures you/they have of the third or fourth child, as opposed to the firstborn.

This is why we need self-discipline. This is why we need character or self-control. Discipline is one of the most productive things that Martial Arts helped to instill in me. I believe, if there were such a thing as a silver bullet of success, it would be self-discipline. Those with self-discipline do more than start a task or project, they follow through to the finish. In any area, when you follow through, you will eventually break through.

This is one reason why I have a coaching program. It is so I can take people by the hand and walk them through the principles I cover. Usually when we do not have someone that we are accountable to, we do not follow through. Perhaps this is why people rarely do what's expected, but often do what they know will be inspected. In fact, all successful people have a coach, a mentor or someone that can work with them. I know that the coaches and mentors I have had in my life, both past and present, have really helped me in every area of life.

My friend, there are people who know different things, who are a little further down the road than you. These people want to help you reach the breakthrough that you desire. Seek them out and let them assist you. Benjamin Franklin was so right when he said, "A man wrapped up in himself makes a very small bundle."

I have developed some other products that assist people in helping them to follow through. When I do my demonstration, I'll call several people up from the audience, as I mentioned, and have them punch me in the stomach, or elbow me, or kick me. It's amazing, because I tell the audience to watch carefully. They notice as the people hit me that it bounces right off of me. The elbows bounce right off. The feet bounce right off. Recently, while speaking in London, England, a 6'9", 320-pound man kicked me with such force with a roundhouse kick that he bounced off my stomach and landed on the floor. The crowd went wild.

I have allowed martial artists to do their spinning kicks on me. I even allowed a football player who was 370 pounds to get in his stance and charge me; he hit me with his shoulder. The force of the impact pushed us both back a few steps. Relax, there were no injuries. Actually, my stomach muscles are so developed that people are amazed!

What is the point or principle? When I was a 6-year-old boy and the teenage gang members hit me in my stomach, my body absorbed all of the shock, thus it knocked the air out of me.

Now, after many years of practice, physical training and mental conditioning, I am prepared, and to date I have withstood 1 million hits to my stomach without sustaining a single injury.

We learned years ago that there is always someone better or stronger. Thus, I always pray before my demonstrations and ask, "Please Lord, do not let them show up today." (smile)

I do this as an illustration to show my audience how, years ago, what used to knock the air out of me, now just bounces off. Many times, I jokingly say, "Would you like to try again," or I say, "Is that the hardest you can hit?"

Warning, do not try this - Houdini the magician died years ago from a punch to the stomach when he was not ready.

I am not trying to lift myself up. I want you to get the point that our weakness can become our strength. As human beings, we can increase, we can grow, and we can accomplish a lot more than we are aware of at this point in our lives. I have developed some training materials that when you implement them, you literally can grow as a person. You can grow to the place where the thing that used to knock the air out of you will just bounce right off.

You can grow as a person to the point where the thing that caused you so much pain will not even cause you to flinch. It will be like water off a duck's back.

I challenge you. If you need help in this area of follow-through, I challenge you to allow me to assist you in following through so you can experience the breakthroughs that you desire, that you deserve.

You know you want it badly, very badly. One reason you are reading this book is that you are ready to stop talking about breakthroughs. You are now ready to experience them!

Sir Edmund Hillary tried to climb Mt. Everest but was unsuccessful the first time. While giving a speech, he pointed to Mt. Everest and said, "Mountain you beat me, but the day will come when I will defeat you."

He said, "You are as big as you will ever be. I, on the other hand, am still growing. I will defeat you one day."

As you guessed, he climbed Mt. Everest just as you will Break Through when you commit to your own personal growth and development.

"The largest room in the world is the room for personal development."

A true business is really a personal development course disguised as a business. The more you grow as an individual, the more effective you will be in business.

In order to accomplish things you've never done before, you have to grow into the person you've never been before.

While speaking, I often close with this powerful poem by Berton Bradley.

The Will To Win

If you want a thing bad enough to go out and fight for it,
Work day and night for it,
Give up your time your peace and your sleep for it.

If all that you scheme and you dream is about it,
If life seems all empty and useless without it.

If gladly you'll sweat for it,
Fret for it, Plan for it,
Lose all your terror of God and man for it,

If you simply go after that thing that you want,
With all your capacity,
Strength and sagacity,
Faith, hope and confidence, stern pertinacity,

If neither cold poverty, famished and gaunt,
Nor sickness nor pain, of body or brain
Can turn you away from the thing that you want,

If dogged and grim you besiege and beset it,
With the help of Almighty God,
You will get it!

It is time for me to break free!

www.JoinDrBreakThrough.com

CHAPTER 7

FASTING

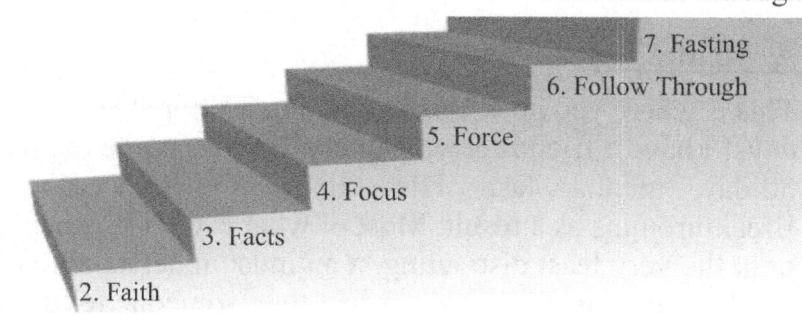

Your Break Through

7. Fasting
6. Follow Through
5. Force
4. Focus
3. Facts
2. Faith
1. Forgive

Step Seven Is Fasting.

The final step to the Guaranteed Break Through Formula is something that few people know about. Yet, those who practice the principle of fasting in its various forms, experience real power and a serious Break Through. Fasting forces us to let go of the visible in order to grab hold of the invisible. It is when the tangible is released that we get a better grasp of the intangible. I dare say that fasting is the key that will open the door to your Break Through. Fasting restores our discipline; it allows us to grab hold of greater things. There is a spiritual principle of releasing what you want, so that it will be free to come to you. (read that again)

People who are serious about experiencing a massive Breakthrough have often used fasting (doing without). I have practiced fasting for over 33 years, all the way from a single meal, to 102 days on nothing but water and juice.

I can tell you that you are bound for a breakthrough when you are serious enough to fast. Let me cover three areas or types of fasts that will assist you tremendously.

A. Mental Fast

This is where you go without watching TV for at least 21 - 30 days! I have a friend Jerry, who challenges people to go on a 30-day mental fast. His clients experience serious Breakthroughs as a result. Most of what is on TV is negative or at the very least distracting. You must understand that the (Tell -a -Vision) Television is just that, someone telling you their vision. Get busy accomplishing your own visions.

Advertisers spend billions of dollars to capture and arrest your attention in order to sell their goods. TV is a form of amusement, which literally means not to think (a -no / muse-think). I call TV, *"The plug in drug."* The more TV people watch the less they read. The more people read books, the less TV they watch. Therefore, I want you to give up TV for 21-30 days since you are serious about breaking through!

The TV has been called the, *"Electronic Income Reducer."* If you need a financial or business breakthrough...here are the guidelines, no TV, especially the late night news! Most news is bad, depressing and harmful for your mental health and attitude. Read 15-30 minutes of a powerful or uplifting book daily. Listen to an uplifting CD or watch one of my DVD's listed in the product section on www.DrBreakThrough.com.

Drink plenty of water and use a calendar to keep track. Tell a friend so they can hold you accountable. Agree to pay them $5 if you slip and watch TV (Electronic Income Reducer). Send an Email to DrBreakThrough@gmail.com.

Type "Mental Fast" in the subject line and I will send you a gift when you complete your task. My life has been transformed by mental fasting. I believe your life will change as well. So fill out the commitment form, and get started now!

I _____ give up TV for _____ days

Beginning _____ and ending _____ .

Signed_____ Dated _____

Witness _____ Dated _____

****

B. Meat Fast - Daniel 1:8-15

This fast (10 days of no meat) goes a step beyond the previous, or if you like, you may combine the two. I have had hundreds of people participate in this type of fast with almost miraculous results! Our bodies really were not created to eat meat, nor were our teeth. Adam, the original man, was vegetarian, along with all of the animals.

Pork is a real no, no, although it used to be my favorite. Once I learned that the pig is a scavenger, which really boils down to being the earth's garbage disposal, I never ate another bite. Pigs do not sweat, contrary to the old saying "sweat like a pig." Thus, all the garbage/toxins that they eat stay within, only to be consumed by unknowing humans. If you need a Breakthrough, especially in the area of your health, give up pork for 10, 21, 30 days or like I have done, forever.

Red meat is bad for you. When John Wayne died, they found 70 lbs of waste in his colon! Our digestive systems just cannot handle breaking down beef. Believe me; I used to eat meat as much, if not more, than the average person did. But once I started learning about how damaging it is to our system, I gave it up. Oprah Winfrey found out what they fed cows to make them fat and decided never to eat beef again. I stopped eating meat in 1996 for 10 days at a time; it has turned into 5,110 days (14 years). I am not sure how much longer I will do this, but I can tell you I no longer desire meat, and my energy and endurance has increased tremendously!

Chicken is harmful as well. The growth hormones are especially affecting our children. Girls are now hitting puberty at such early ages that it is shocking. Men are growing breasts (some get breast cancer), and women are experiencing serous hormonal problems. The mercury content is just too high in fish today. You need to study this for yourself. It will shock you. When I first gave up flesh, I thought I would grow weak but I've actually gotten stronger! Come on now, just give it 10, 21 or 30 days and see what happens. You probably will detoxify and/or experience headaches and sluggishness for a few days. Be sure to double up on your water and supplement intake.

C. Miracle Fast - Mark 9:29

This kind can come forth by nothing, but by prayer and fasting! Now when you really need a serious Breakthrough commit to a 1, 3, 7, 10 or 21 day fast and you may experience things just short of a miracle! Currently, I have been on a fast for the last 102 days while writing this because I always want to live my message! (Caution, please do not attempt to fast this long.) I have many years of experience and have been under a physician's care while on this Break Through fast. I can tell you that a 1-day, 3-day or 7-day fast will often bring great results. Please consult a physician before you do a fast to make sure that you are healthy enough.

Fasting has been known to have awesome benefits including weight loss, (I lost 100 pounds in 102 days), better mental clarity and focus, increased spiritual awareness, more personal discipline and power, etc. I have experienced all of these benefits and more! I have a new house, an extra $30,000 consulting bonus, and I recently (5/15/09) married Nadia, the woman of my dreams. She was another motivation for fasting so long as I sought divine guidance as to whether we were right for each other. We travel together and we started a contest to see who will love each other the most. I think I am winning. I guess you will have to ask her to see if she agrees. If you need a Break Through in your relationship, fasting may be the key. History is full of examples of people in great need and distress that engaged in fasting and had wonderful results.

I train on self-control/self-discipline. I produced a CD and I have a free report on the "silver bullet of success - self discipline." I know of no better way of increasing your discipline than fasting.

We all experience information overload at times. What we really need is a renewed commitment toward implementing what we have learned.

Now let me ask you a question. How bad do you want your breakthrough? Do you want it enough that you would be willing to do a 21-30 day mental fast? Are you willing to do a meat fast or even a miracle fast?

Successful people always ask this question, "Is it worth it?" Is your breakthrough worth it? Do not answer with your lips but rather your life. I believe you are serious, now show me that I was right in my assessment of you.

This powerful 7-step formula is like a bomb that can blast or break through whatever you are facing. Keep in mind one very crucial point. Regardless of how potent or powerful a bomb is, until it is set off or detonated, nothing happens.

The speed of your implementation will determine the speed you break through to your success. Please read that again.

I am your Breakthrough coach and I believe in you. If you need further assistance as many do, let me take you further with my Breakthrough Coaching program designed with your Breakthrough in mind. The question is not how much does it cost, but rather, "Is it worth it?" I believe and know so, but only you can answer for yourself. I am here to help. Successful people ask, "is it worth it," not "is it easy/cheap?"

Breakthrough Fasting Tips

1. Find a friend or two to fast with you! It makes fasting easier! You derive strength and support from each other. The good book says, "Two are better than one." You have multiplied power when you have others in a common bond. If two on earth shall agree as touching anything, it shall be done…. If you want to go on a long fast, ask a friend to fast the first day with you. Ask friend B to fast the second day. Invite friend C to fast the third, etc.

2. Take several enemas before and during your fast. This will help clean out the waste, which literally could be re-absorbed into your system, thus causing headaches, dizziness or a white coating on your tongue, etc. A colonic (hydrotherapy) is sort of like a high-powered enema and if you have the money, they work 10 times better than an enema. My whole family has had several. I highly recommend them. Imagine taking an internal bath, it will greatly benefit your organs. I know you cleaned up today, but when is the last time you got cleaned out?

3. Read books on fasting, listen to CD's, sermons etc. on this or a similar topic. It is imperative that you do this to ensure your success. It will help focus your mind, inspire your soul, and strengthen your resolve.

4. Prepare for attacks! Your mind will tell you "you're starving." Your addictions (smoking, coffee, soda, sugar etc.) will cause your body to go through withdrawals. Do not back down and give in to the temptation to eat! Well meaning friends and family will say "stop starving yourself, you could die." When you fast, you may even experience a healing crisis. Rashes, pimples, aches and pains often signify that the body is repairing long overdue projects. You see, we live on such little nutrition that the body only has enough energy to survive. However, fasting allows the body to go back and repair itself.

5. Get plenty of rest; take an extra 10-30 minute power nap. Do some deep cleansing and relaxing breaths. Inhale through your nose, hold it tor 5 seconds then exhale out your mouth very slowly. Use your diaphragm (stomach), not your chest.

6. Drink carrot juice mixed with a little apple, or go all out and get a juicer and make fresh organic juice daily. This will actually energize you beyond your wildest dreams. This is how I fasted 52 days several years ago and more recently 102 days! I am now starting a 40 day fast.

7. Refocus your attention from food or hunger to your goal! As your bodies cries out for food, cry out for your Break Through! Pray and ask the Lord to give you power. Check out www.FreeFromDrBreakThrough.com to listen to and watch some free empowering messages that will encourage and equip you with strength for your journey.

Get ready for the third part, which consists of barriers to which you will be familiar. Sadly, some people would rather stay with a familiar problem than embrace an unfamiliar solution. People often resist change until the pressure or pain is great enough. Most people are motivated by fear of loss, pain or desire for reward. With this in mind, allow me to familiarize you with solutions that will empower you to break through these barriers and gain several rewards while avoiding great loss.

While Speaking in Alaska

I've been told that I could sell ice to an Eskimo (smile).

It is time for me to break free!

PART III:

THE FAMILIAR

The final set of chapters are based upon things I often write on boards before I break through them, showing the audience a physical illustration of the psychological effect that my message will have on them.

If you were to ask 100 people if they could identify with the things that I will cover, 100 of them will identify with these barriers. When we speak about things like fear, doubt, procrastination, lack of discipline etc., we all are familiar with these.

By the way, the pain of discipline seems small compared to the pain of regret.

Therefore, this is why I call this final section, "The Familiar." Successful people learn to break through barriers while others shrink back and become mediocre. God intended for all of us to become champions. Champions face challenges and learn to overcome them. So get prepared as we deal with the barriers that many are familiar with, but have not had a mentor to show them how to break through.

It is time for me to break free!

www.DrBreakThrough.com

Josh and I have learned to lean on one another.

"People Are Like Books"-Joshua Harris

People are like books
Environment and experience are the pen,
our memories provide the paper,
and their blood, sweat, and tears constitute the ink.

People are like books,
and they are just begging,
and sometimes demanding,
for someone to read them.
Only the incredibly brave
or incredibly stupid
dare be illiterate
in this day-and-age

But then -
fools rush in where angels fear to tread"...

CHAPTER 1

BAD HEALTH

If you really want to be wealthy, you cannot just have money, you have to have your health. Many people need a breakthrough in the area of their health.

I was out of balance several years ago. I was overzealous, I used to travel 320 days a year. Yes, you read that right. I still love to travel with my sweet wife, but obviously, I do not travel as much as I did in my overzealous past.

I was overzealous and wanted to prove to the world that I was a young, black man that was not lazy. Did you know that men who grow up without the approval of their fathers usually become type-A overachievers? They become driven!

I am glad that when I turned 17, and got a car, I reconnected with my dad. I found out where he lived and we started a relationship. Years later, he attended my college graduation. One day he told me that he was proud of me, as his oldest son, and that he was proud of my accomplishments. He has traveled to hear me speak a few times—what a powerful relationship Break Through. You can have one as well!

As I stated previously, I was way out of balance, averaging only four hours of sleep per night. I did that for about 18 years of my life. I started that insane schedule in college where I took a full load, and worked two jobs to pay my own way through college.

I remember hearing a man talk about going to college and working a full-time job. I thought to myself as a young teenager, "How in the world could you work a full-time job and go to school full time?" Well, I went to school full time, worked a full-time job and a part-time job simultaneously. It is amazing what you can achieve if you want it bad enough.

During my days of traveling, 320 days per year, I eventually collapsed out of exhaustion. I woke up with a doctor looking at me, and I did not know what happened or how I got there. At this time, I was 36 years old and I was the Pennsylvania Tri-State Champion of Martial Arts.

At the time, I assumed that because I looked okay, I was healthy. Sadly, we have seen the stories of perfect V-cut athletes who dropped over dead with heart attacks, etc.

Many of you need a breakthrough in your health. I was never aware of it before, but as I mentioned earlier, your pain can turn into your power. Pain can push you to prosperity. Pain causes some to break, while others break records!

At 36, it appeared that I had a stroke and a nervous condition. They did a burnout inventory test, and I tested two points higher than anyone they had previously tested. I was a mess physically, mentally and psychologically.

I went through a deep, dark depression and became suicidal for a while. I literally was almost like a vegetable, emotionally wrecked and physically exhausted. It was as if the flame of my life blew out. I was at the lowest point of my life and desperately in need of a major Break Through!

Literally, what they found out was that I was running off adrenaline, I had exhausted my adrenal glands, my body simply shut down.

Today, I am strong and vibrant. I allowed my pain to push me to learn some principles that allowed and assisted me to have a breakthrough in my health.

If you are suffering from depression (not chronic), as many have, drink three glasses of water consecutively. Yes, I said three glasses of water consecutively and several throughout the day and see what happens. In over 80% of the time, people would tell me the symptoms of depression fade, or disappear.

I believe a lot of our depression comes from dehydration. The first thing that dehydrates is the brain cells, it messes up the neurotransmitters and that drops us into a state of depression. Literally, by drinking three glasses of water (and several more throughout the day) the cells have an unusual ability to function once properly hydrated.

I just want to throw that tip at you. You need to seek the help of your physician in that type of situation, but in many cases, drinking water will help you. www.BreakThroughWater.com

I came up with what I call *"The 5 Essentials for Ultimate Health."* I want you to read and consider them.

1. Attitude

When we talk about attitude, a good attitude is an attitude of gratitude. My friend Zig Ziglar says, "Most people have stinking thinking." What are you grateful for today? Make a list of 10 things you will give thanks for over the next 21 days. You ought to give thanks every meal/day.

Many people are not grateful. If they would experience being grateful, they would experience a higher degree of energy, health and abundance. Everywhere I go people think I'm a whole lot younger than I am. They ask me, "How do you have so much energy?" This is part of my secret, I maintain a good attitude, I make sure that I give thanks, and I enjoy laughing.

2. Activities

• Laughter

Years ago, Norman Cousins got sick and was told he would die soon. He read a phrase that changed his life forever. *"A merry heart doeth good like a medicine,"* Proverbs 17:22 He hired a bunch of clowns to come to his hospital room and keep him laughing. He got several clips of the old TV show called "Candid Camera."

He literally laughed himself back to health. He also took some mega doses of vitamin C. Years later, some universities did studies and found out that when we laugh, it literally opens up the endorphins. They discovered that laughter has medicinal purposes.

Laugh often and do not take life too seriously, you cannot get out alive, so enjoy while you're here (smile). I noticed before my collapse that I was super-serious and I would not take a vacation. I thought I had to get everything done on time.

I am telling you, if you want a breakthrough in your health, you have to learn how to have an attitude of gratitude. You have to learn to laugh and enjoy life, and just do not sweat the small stuff.

• Exercise

Learn to exercise and do it daily. Although I did some exercise, aerobic exercise is the best at keeping down those stress levels and keeping your heart healthy.

Many times, the older we get, the less we exercise. Just walking is such a powerful exercise. You can walk and give thanks. Walking with a friend and/or spouse can enhance your relationship

By the way, it is amazing that if you're in a relationship and you walk with that person, you will notice that your steps tend to synchronize and be in harmony. I like to walk and pray, walk while I sing and think. You can walk with vigor by pumping your arms and taking longer, quicker steps. A treadmill works great, do some jumping jacks, pushups etc.

3. Alkalizing Food

Learn to get away from the double F's. What I mean is fast foods, "food-less foods" and the "fiber-less foods."

That is one reason why in America we have many overweight people who constantly eat, but they are not satisfied. They're eating "food-less food." There is no nutritional value whatsoever in the food that they are eating, and so the appetite is constantly open. They are just eating filler.

Alkalizing foods are foods that are raw. It's your fruits and your vegetables that will assist your bodies. One of the things we want to do is keep the body in homeostasis (or proper balance), because as long as the body is in proper balance, the body will fix whatever is wrong. God made this body to be totally amazing and self-sufficient. If you cut your arm, it will start to heal naturally.

Oftentimes, because of the stimulants like sugar, caffeine, nicotine, red meat and salt, over consuming these stimulants break the body down and cause the body to be acidic. Your body needs to be 7.2 and the blood needs to be 7.4.

You have to understand something. You have to eat more alkalizing food, more fruits and vegetables. I have people go on a meat fast and cut it out of their diet for a while. I know it sounds impossible to you but it is not, besides they have many meat alternatives such as veggie burgers, veggie bacon, etc.

When I became a vegetarian (vegan for 7 years), my friends thought I would become weak. I asked, "Do you mean weak like a gorilla, a hippopotamus or rhino? These huge, powerful animals are all vegetarians." They would say, "You'll shrivel up to nothing." I replied, "Oh, you mean like an elephant?"

Are you aware that some of the largest animals in the world are vegetarian? Please realize the problem is not meat. The problem is what they do to the animals by injecting them with dangerous and toxic growth hormones.

Chickens are slaughtered in the 8th week. This is done because in the 9th week, many become cancerous, and you can see the cancer sores on them. (This is bad for business)

You may feel like I did when I first learned some of these things, "I can't give this up." At least consider reducing the red meat and pork.

As I stated earlier, you can at least scale back a little bit. I am not telling you that you have to do all of this. I am saying these are things I have done and have reaped great benefits.

I could spar 11 people in a row, and then after becoming a vegetarian, I was able to spar with 22 people in a row (Sparring is fighting in martial arts). I would fight one after another without taking a break.

All my friends said, "Man, you must be on something." I replied, "Yeah, I'm on healthy food."

I was also juicing fruits and vegetables daily. I often paid my children to juice. They all adopted the vegetarian lifestyle by just watching me. Joshua even went through boot camp (Marines) as a vegetarian. It was a lot of work, but I'm telling you it made a huge difference! The Latin root word for vegetarian (vegetare) means to enliven.

The average American in their lifetime will eat 900 Chickens, 24 Hogs, 15 cows, 12 Sheep and 1,000 pounds of fish or other animals. Your digestive system cannot handle this flesh overload. Many people suffer from digestive problems because anything heated has had all the life cooked out of it.

If you are not willing to change what you eat, at least change *when you eat.* There is a revolutionary eating schedule concept called the "Circadian Rhythm" of the body. They say from noon to 8 p.m. is appropriation. That means that is the only time you should appropriate, or take things into the body. Then, from 8 p.m. to 4 a.m. is digestion and assimilation. That is when the body breaks down and assimilates the different nutrients. Then, from 4 a.m. to noon is elimination and cleansing.

That is one reason why they call the first meal of the day breakfast (break-fast, break the fast). If you are going to eat anything for breakfast, it should be something light such as fruit, which assists, in the cleansing process.

Friends of mine who have their own clinics say clients report better health if they just start eating according to this schedule. Just as a farmer knows the best time to plant the crop in order to reap the best harvest, I found for my body that if I eat after 9 p.m., I wake up the next day tired. Why? My digestive system was working, although I was asleep. At any rate, try to eat as much alkalizing, live foods as possible. You cannot get life out of death, nor vitality out of dead food. The standard American diet (S.A.D) is causing many health issues. Anything cooked, baked, fried, or in a can is acidic, disease can only live in an acidic body!

4. Ample amounts of water and rest

Our body is about 80% water. The brain is about 85-90% water. You expel about eight glasses of water every day just by breathing. How does the body replenish the water it lost? When you take a bath/shower, your body absorbs up to 3 pounds of water. Do not believe me, just weigh yourself before you shower than again afterwards and see for yourself. When you inhale, you exhale. If you get close to a mirror, you will notice the fog (water) on the mirror. For years I did not like the taste of water, nor did I understand its importance.

Upon rising, immediately drink a tall glass of purified water. I only drink purified, hexagonal, ionized, alkaline water, which has changed my life! By the way, my 102-day fast was accomplished by using this special water. I felt good during this fast as opposed to other fasts that I have done, and the water was the only difference.

The special Break Through water I use has been purified, and electrically restructured to help the body release excess body fat and toxins.

It is estimated that 75% of Americans are dehydrated to the extent that it affects their everyday health. One of the main causes for daytime fatigue is simply a lack of water. Many people (especially women) experience chronic constipation. Here are a few symptoms of toxic overload: headaches, memory loss, muscle aches, frequent colds and depression.

When depressed, try drinking three glasses of water and see how you feel. Many people feel a lot better simply because the brain cells are getting the needed hydration. Water and good quality supplements are mandatory for good health.

I strongly recommend that you never drink any more tap water because it can contain up to 90 legally allowable chemicals. It also contains chlorine and its by-products, which have been linked to bladder, breast and other cancers. Do not believe me, study for yourself, go to www.BreakThroughWater.com and download your free report, while limited supplies last.

If you weigh 200 pounds, you ought to be drinking 100 ounces every day of water. In other words, take your body weight, cut it in half and convert it to ounces. Now in the beginning, your kidneys may need to adjust. You may have to use the bathroom quite a bit, but they will get used to it after a while. Your urine should be the color of a baby's urine. Most people urinate, a dark yellow color.

The more water you drink, the cleaner your urine will become, this means your body is flushing out the toxins. Every metabolic process of the body requires water. People frequently comment on how clear and supple my skin appears. Well the skin is the largest organ of the body. Drinking plenty of water and taking quality supplements has helped my skin tremendously. Do you desire similar results?

Before my breakdown, I totally underestimated the importance of getting good rest and great sleep. I was like an impatient man who put his car in the shop but took it back out before the mechanics had time to finish the needed repairs.

You must understand that while we sleep, our bodies start repairing themselves, thus it is necessary to get good rest.

This is why forgiveness is so important because many people suffer from sleep disorders and in some cases; it has been traced to a lack of forgiveness. It has been my experience as well as others that anger, resentment and/or not asking and/or extending forgiveness can wreak havoc on your quality of sleep. Pause for a few minutes and ask yourself, "Do I rest well?" If not, are you ready to let go of resentment now? Who do you need to forgive right now (or of whom do you need to ask forgiveness), so that you can sleep tonight? They may not deserve your gift of forgiveness, but your health does.

It is also good to take good health products to supplement your health. I would never go a day without taking good quality health products.

5. Air

We breathe about 23,000 breaths per day. It's amazing that every year, 64,000 people die from airborne particulates, and we're spending 80% of our time indoors! The number one nutrient for the body is clean air. Most people do not even take deep breaths. When is the last time you enjoyed one?

Singers and martial artists understand diaphragmatic breathing. Unlike here in Western culture, where we breathe up in our chest, you want to breathe from your diaphragm. Your belly should come out when you inhale through your nose and exhale from your mouth. You ought to take a few deep breaths every day. Stop right now, close your eyes and breathe in your nose allowing your stomach to fill. Now exhale through your mouth slowly. Did you notice a difference, a calming effect or maybe a release of stress?

Taking 10 to 20 cleansing breaths, breathing in, holding it for a couple of seconds and then breathing out will help you in your health, and lower your stress levels. Learn to get outside a little more and breathe nice, clean air.

It is also good to have some type of air purification system in your home. I will never be without one, and I have had them in my home(s) for over 13 years. You have one of two choices and your health depends on you making the right choice.

You can either buy a purifier or become a purifier.

Buying one will cost you some wealth, becoming one will cost your health.

May I remind you that if you lose your health, your wealth will not matter? Do you want to become an air purifier or buy an air purifier?

I want you to understand that these are key elements that will assist you in your journey to better health. It is an amazing thing that we do not take better care of our health.

Without your health, nothing else will matter, except getting your health back. So take some good preventative steps now. Sadly enough, when you ignore your health, it will go away, and take your money, and perhaps your honey with it!

If you have a breakthrough in your health and experience vibrant energy, this will also assist you in having breakthroughs in every other area of life. The time to start is now, I mean right now, because tomorrow may be too late.

I really want to drive home the fact that after my collapse, I subtracted the bad from my diet but equally as important, I added good things to my diet and lifestyle.

You need to know that even our fruits and vegetables are lacking some nutrients because the soil has been depleted, and they pick the crops early in order to ship them out.

This means the plants do not get a chance to get fully ripe, which is when the nutrient content is at its highest.

Please list seven things you will change as a result of reading this section. (Example, I will start taking supplements daily.)

1)_____

2)_____

3)_____

4)_____

5)_____

6)_____

7)_____

It is time for me to break free!

CHAPTER 2

BEING POOR

My acronyms for poor:

P	-	*Putting*
O	-	*Obstacles*
O	-	*Over*
R	-	*Riches*

OR

P	-	*Putting*
O	-	*Obstacles*
O	-	*Over*
R	-	*Results*

It's okay to be broke because the average millionaire has experienced being broke (not poor) 2.3 times. This means that if you have ever been broke, you are well on your way to becoming a millionaire ☺

Sometimes you cannot help but be broke. Broke is a temporary situation; poor is a state of mind. If you are broke, I can help you. If you are poor, I cannot help you. Poor people like to be victims. They have to break through the poverty mentality to a prosperity mentality.

The only difference between a man/woman with money and a man/woman who does not have money is that the one who does not have money came to an obstacle and said, "It's too hard, I can't do this."

The one who has money came to the same obstacle and said, "I'm going over, under, around, or with Dr. Break Through's help, I'm going to go through this obstacle."

Have you ever wondered why people make extra money then end up being just as broke? People who win the lottery end up being broke within two years, even if they have won millions. Why is this true? Because, if you do not grow to the level of your money, it will shrink to the level of your character.

Many people liken your financial blueprint to a thermostat. If it is set subconsciously for example at $40,000 a year and you make $100,000 you will sabotage yourself to go back down to $40,000. This is why you need to reprogram your thought process concerning money and abundance with my *Break Through Declaration* or *Daily Attitude Adjuster*.

I was speaking at a church and someone said to me, "But didn't Jesus say the poor you have with you always?"

I said, "Yes, but He didn't say you had to be one of them."

In fact, the best way to help the poor is not to be one of them.

I have been poor and I have been rich, and rich is a whole lot better than being poor. Someone said, "I thought that the Bible says that <u>money</u> is the root of all evil." <u>No</u>, it is the love of money that is the root of all kinds of evil. Some people who do not have it *love it more* than those who have it. In fact, those who do not have it think about it more than those who have money. Now think about that statement for a while.

I often explain in my seminar, although the love of money is the root of all evil, the lack of money is the manifestation of evil. The man who tries to steal your car or break into your home is not the one with money, but rather the one who lacks money.

I am telling you that some people in life are hurting and have real needs. It is one thing for someone to come to you with a need and you respond, "I feel sorry for you." Maybe you even pray for them, but you are powerless to do anything to physically help them and make a significant difference.

I have asked people this question. If you have a financial need and you come to me and want me to pray with you about a certain bill, I can pray with you, and then we can stop there. On the other hand, would you prefer I pray with you and then give you some help with your bill?

Now, obviously you and I cannot help everyone because sometimes help can hurt people. Help hurts people if they become dependent on the help, or if it hinders them from learning the needed lessons of life.

It is a great joy when someone comes to you with a legitimate need for transportation and you can actually take them down to the car lot and purchase a car for them. I have been able to purchase a car on two occasions for people (other than my children). I say this not to lift myself up, because if I did not have it at the time, I could not have helped in that way.

Actually, I tell people money is not everything, but it is kind of like oxygen. You feel like you would die without it. Money cannot buy happiness, but it is a good down payment! It gives you options that you would not have otherwise.

I personally do not need money, but every time I go to the gas station, guess what they want? Every time I go to the grocery store, they will not let me have any groceries unless I give them money. Many things I have to do cannot be done without money. I often say, "I don't need money. The bill collector needs money. The mortgage and insurance agent needs money. I do not need it. But, since I'm the person in charge, I have to have it to take care of the needs."

Eccl. 7:12 says, *"Money is a defense."* I teach a course and have a CD set on *Financial Self Defense.* I learned self defense to protect myself physically. However, we equally need to learn to protect ourselves financially and not depend on others to bail us out. Realistically, there are only two people who care about your bills; you and the person you owe! (smile)

I have a serious problem with people who want just enough money for them to get by. How selfish is that? You should have enough to help yourself and others. Solomon said, *"Money answereth all things,"* Eccl. 10:12.

My wife and I have a goal to support 100 missionaries. I do not think a missionary should have to travel around for three or four years asking churches to support them, so they can go and do what God has called them to do. I believe they should be able to go and get the good news out as soon as possible.

If you have taken a vow of poverty, I respect your oath; I just want to free those who mistakenly thought they were included in your vow.

Poverty mentality people say, "Well, you can't have your cake and eat it too." I tell people, "If I can't eat the cake, I don't want it." I want my cake, so I can eat it and then have some ice cream, take vitamins and exercise. The choice is not either/or, but rather both/and (bad grammar, but a great message). We ought to have an abundance mentality instead of a poverty mentality. When you experience your financial breakthrough, you will never be the same again! These scriptures can help.

Job 36:11, "If they obey and serve Him, they shall spend their days in prosperity and their years in pleasures."

Psalms 1:3, "And whatsoever he doeth shall prosper."

Psalms 112:3, "Wealth and riches shall be in his house."

Psalms 115:14,15, "The Lord shall increase you more and more, you and your children, for ye are blessed of the Lord."

Proverbs 8:21, "That I may cause those that love me to inherit substance, and I will fill their treasures."

Proverbs 10:4, "He becometh poor that dealeth with a slack hand, but the hand of the diligent maketh rich."

Proverbs 10:22, "The blessing of the Lord, it maketh rich and He addeth no sorrow with it."

Proverbs 15:6, "In the house of the righteous is much treasure."

Isaiah 45:3, "And I will give thee the treasures of darkness and hidden riches of secret places."

Mark 10:30, "But he shall receive a hundredfold, now in this time, houses and brethren and lands."

Romans 8:32, "He that spared not his own Son, but delivered him up for us all, how shall he not with him also freely give us all things?"

Mark 11:23, "For verily I say unto you, that whosoever shall say unto this mountain, be thou removed, and be thou cast into the sea, and shall not doubt in his heart, but shall believe that those things which he saith shall come to pass, he shall have whatsoever he saith."

Philippians 4:13, "I can do all things through Christ who strengthens me."

I want you to read these statements aloud, and add your name.

- Today, I _____ look forward to enjoying abundant energy, health and wealth.

- I _____ embrace abundance and it embraces me. I am an abundance magnet!

- I _____ use money to help myself and others. Money likes me, it is attracted to me, and it comes to me abundantly from many places.

- I _____ now release the financial champion that is inside of me!

Now if you repeat these daily for 30 days, you can re-record over your old financial blueprint and reset it to a higher level of financial success. (If you did not fill your name in the blanks, get a pen and do it now before you go any further.)

I used to feel a little guilty if I made a lot of money, now I realize that if you give good value, you deserve to receive value in return. *The level of awareness of your self-worth, will ultimately determine the level or amount of your net-worth.*

I once asked one of my main business mentors, Bill Bailey (www.WilliamEBailey.com), what he did to make $64 million a month with his company way back in the 70's. He replied, "Dr. Stan, you're asking the wrong question." I said,

"Okay, I apologize. What would be the right question?" He said, "You should have asked me, how many people's lives I added value to that resulted in $64 million per month?" He then made his final powerful point, "You see Dr. Stan, if you give great value, you cannot stop the value from returning." He said it has been said by one far greater than me, "*give and it shall be given unto you, good measure, pressed down, shaken together and running over shall men give into your bosom*" (Luke 6:38).

Enjoying Some of Life's Blessings

When I was voted into the Black belt Hall of fame

I didn't become a champion by staying in my Comfort Zone!

CHAPTER 3

COMFORT ZONE

Comfort zone is a thing that we need to break out of in order to step into our greatness (which awaits us). This is often the barrier between where we are and where we would like to be, the problem is that we want to get to that place as comfortably as we possibly can and that just will not happen.

You must understand that risk is the ledge that gives winners the edge. You have to break out of your comfort zone, because life begins at the end of your comfort zone. Did you get that? Life begins at _____ _____ _____ _____ _____ _____! (Please fill in the blanks now, as you say it aloud.)

Many times, we are in a comfort zone and we want to stay there. Nevertheless, if we are going to have a breakthrough and accomplish great things we must come out of our comfort zones.

I was talking to a person recently. I said, "Most people, not just young people, but middle-aged people as well, would rather be the best of the worst than the worst of the best." In other words, they would like to be the best person in the group. They do this so they can feel comfortable and feel good because they're at the top of everything.

When I started in the martial arts 41 years ago, I said I wanted to hang with the best Karate-ka (practitioner of the art) in the class. I decided to work out with him. When it came time for sparring, which is fighting in the martial arts, I would match up with him. Of course, he easily beat me.

My skill level rapidly increased. I was the worst of the best, because I hung out with the Black Belts and sparred against them consistently. Whenever I was matched against a white or green belt, they were little if any competition.

Instead of being the best of the worst, I was the worst of the best, and that raised my skill level immensely. If I had just hung out with the white belts, perhaps I could have beaten all of them; that would only make me the best of the worst. That would have been in my comfort zone. Because I was able to stretch outside of my comfort zone, I went from being the worst of the best to eventually becoming the best of the best. Those who chose the easy route of being the best of the worst, are still just that, the best of the worst.

One day I learned to block the guy that used to beat me. Another day I learned to strike back. Years later, I actually got to the point where I could beat him sparring. I cannot explain how happy I felt that day. I have since learned to compete against my own record and to better myself daily.

You have to come out of your comfort zone to experience a breakthrough. Outside of your comfort zone is not fun but it is very rewarding in the end. Imagine a football player who gets the ball and the opposing team just moves out of his way so he can run a touchdown. That would actually destroy the very essence and point of the game. Without opposition, anyone can run down the field, but it would be meaningless.

Please get this! Powerful people have learned to be comfortable with being uncomfortable - why? Because we usually only grow and accomplish things when we are uncomfortable. You have to get to the place that you do not mind being put into an uncomfortable place or position because that is where your hidden greatness will surface. A grain of sand in an oyster is very uncomfortable, but in the end, it forms into a beautiful pearl of great beauty and worth.

Put a speaker on the spot and often, they will give their best speech. Here is why, when put on the spot, speakers speak from their heart (source of power) instead of their head (source of thought). I have since learned to speak from both my head and my heart for optimum effectiveness.

Comfort Zone

I used to have a comfort zone, where I knew I could not fail.
The same four walls and busy work were really more like jail.
I longed so much to do the things I'd never done before,
But I stayed inside my comfort zone and paced the same old
*   floor.*

I said it didn't matter that I wasn't doing much.
I said I didn't care for things like diamonds, cars or such.
I claimed to be so busy with the things inside my zone.
But deep inside I longed for some sweet victory of my own

I couldn't let my life go by, just watching others win.
I held my breath and stepped outside to let the change begin.
I took a step, and with a strain I'd never felt before,
I kissed my comfort zone goodbye and closed and locked the
*   door.*

If you are in a comfort zone afraid to venture out,
Remember that all winners at one time were filled with doubt,
A step or two and words of praise can make your dreams
*   come true,*
So greet your future with a smile, success is there for you!

-Author Unknown

A great leader and orator said to the people, "Come to the edge." They responded, "We are afraid we may fall." He said with more vigor, "Come to the edge." They replied, "We are afraid." He replied with a loud, deep, commanding voice, "Come to the edge now!" So, they came. He pushed them, and to their surprise, they grew wings on the way down, and they flew!

"Two of my mentors who inspired me to fly higher."

Left to right: "Jim Rohn, Dr. Break Through, Bill Bailey"

It is time for me to break free!

CHAPTER 4

DISEMPOWERING QUESTIONS & STATEMENTS

Disempowering denotes no power left, to surrender or to give your power away.

An example of a disempowering question is when something bad happens and you ask, "Why me?"

My question is, "Do you have anyone better in mind?"

Years ago, I learned to stop asking, "Why me?" I learned to ask, "What are you trying to teach me?" I ask, "What can I learn from this, or through this?" Life will teach you lessons if you are open to learn. If not, you will repeat the same lesson(s), repeatedly.

Learn to ask empowering questions. For instance, "How can I turn this seemingly bad thing into a good thing? How can I overcome this? What resources do I have that can allow me to break through this?" Ask more how vs. why questions. Ask, "When?" or, "How soon?"

Learn to ask great "what if" questions such as: "What if everything turns around? What if I accomplish all of my goals and dreams? What if I could handle anything life throws my way and more? What if I operated in faith and confidence instead of fear and doubt? What if anything good that can happen, does happen and what if it happens at the best possible time?"

It has been wisely stated, "The quality of your life will be determined by the quality of the questions you ask God, yourself, and others" Powerful people ask empowering questions, others ask disempowering questions.

Here is an empowering question. "What would you attempt to do if you knew that you couldn't fail? How would you respond if you were as strong and as awesome as the person you respect the most?"

Have you ever made a similar statement? "So and so makes me sick, they make me so mad, they made me…" Please note that no one can make you do anything, you simply react to them or allow them to push your buttons, but you are in control unless you decide to lose control, or give it to another.

God made you with the most powerful thing in the world, a free will, thus ultimately the choice is yours to give your power to another, or keep it. Eleanor Roosevelt said it best, "No one can make you feel inferior without your consent." Stop giving your power away. Stop playing the victim.

It's been said, "the smartest man/woman in the world only uses 10% of their brain capacity." May I ask a pointed question, "What capacity of your will are you exercising, and what percentage have you given to another?" You were made to have dominion, not to be dominated. *Stop allowing yourself, to be less than yourself!*

I cannot help but close out with the poem that has strengthened many a weary traveler. Soak and bask in the strength that it gives, read it twice and think. Get ready to read one of the most empowering set of words ever penned. If every person going through hard times would heed these words, they would receive strength beyond explanation.

Nelson Mandela quoted these words to himself and others while he was locked up unjustly for 30 years. His captors did everything they could to break his will, but they were unsuccessful.

After gaining his freedom, Nelson Mandela became president, but not just a president, the first African president in turbulent South Africa.

To the utter surprise of many whites and blacks, he did not retaliate against the racism that he and his people suffered for many years, instead he showed great compassion, and true leadership. Instead of the predicted riots, the country became greater under Nelson Mandela's leadership simply because he ruled his own soul; it qualified him to guide others to the highest good of the country. Plato was quoted as saying, "The greatest of all victories is the conquest of one's own self."

"Invictus"

By William Ernest Henley

Out of the night, that covers me,
Black as the pit from pole to pole.
I thank whatever gods may be,
For my unconquerable soul.

In the fell clutch of circumstance,
I have not winced nor cried aloud,
Under the bludgeoning of chance,
My head is bloody, but unbowed.

Beyond this place of wrath and tears,
Looms but the horror of the shade.
And yet the menace of the years,
Finds and shall find me unafraid.

It matters not how strait the gate,
How charged with punishments the scroll.
I am the master of my fate:
I am the captain of my soul!

About to Break Comfort Zone

Various Breaks Including Doubt

CHAPTER 5

DOUBT

Doubt is something that all people without exception need to break through. I love to expound on the fact that people who are walking in their power are people who believe their beliefs and doubt their doubts. Those who have not yet walked in their power doubt their beliefs and believe their doubts. There is a huge difference between walking in doubt and walking in belief.

Before I do a demonstration and/or I speak, doubt creeps in and tries to tell me, "These people aren't going to like you."

Doubt says, "You're going to hurt yourself doing this demonstration."

Doubt says, "You're getting a little older and you need to slow down a bit. You're still going at the same pace, so something bad might happen."

Doubt says, "They're not going to buy any of your products."

Doubt says, "You won't be invited back."

Doubt says, "They may say, 'Boo!' as you speak and ask you to stop and sit down."

I only have one of two choices. Either I can believe, or I can doubt. Which do you think I select? You are correct. I doubt those negative thoughts.

In other words, I have doubt, but I can only do one of two things. I can believe my doubt, or I can doubt my doubt. If I doubt my doubt, I neutralize its power. Consequently, I doubt the doubt to zap its influence. Wow, now that's good stuff!

Before I speak or do a demonstration, belief kicks in and says, "They're going to love you."

Belief says, "You're going to do your demonstration, and every board and brick will break. Everything's going to go very smoothly, and people are going to say, 'How in the world could a man his age do all these things?'"

Belief says, "They're going to love you. They are going to invite you to speak at other places. They are going to buy all of your products. You're going to sell out of all of your CDs, DVDs, books and coaching programs!"

Even as I was preparing this book, belief kicked in and said, "It's going to be a bestseller. People are going to buy this book. They are going to love it. They are going to share it with their friends. They are going to buy many more copies, and give them as gifts. They are going to tell many people about this book. You are going to be invited to speak many more places, you will be invited to do more TV and radio interviews"

I only have one of two choices. I can believe, or I can doubt. What do you think I will do about those thoughts? You are right if you guessed that I would believe them.

The reason is simple, when I believe my beliefs, I give life to my beliefs, and I give more power to them. Literally, as you read these pages, you are feeling the power of congruency.

Congruency means, what I say or write, I also believe and feel. Some people are incongruent. They think and say one thing yet they feel something totally different.

This is one reason why people who may not have a positive message, but they really believe in what they are doing to the depths of their soul and they say what they believe, tend to have more results than people who have a good message, but perhaps have allowed doubt to break down their message.

I will take an unpolished speaker any day who really believes in what they say over a polished speaker who merely speaks. My first choice would be to have the polished speaker who speaks what they believe. Doubt will try to invade you. Doubt is not the problem; it is your response to it. Maybe you believed that you could write a book, and then someone said, "Who are you to write a book? You do not have a doctor's degree. You are not super educated. No one would buy the book if you wrote it. Why waste your time?"

And what did you do? You believed your doubt, and that's why you haven't written your book, produced your CD/DVD, or launched your business.

Maybe something inside of you said, "You should be a public speaker, you should get some training, and maybe you should contact Dr. Break Through and allow him to train you to be a speaker, get some of his materials and allow yourself to learn." That was your belief.

You believed you could become a speaker, but then your doubt came in and you said, "Well, who would want to hear me speak? I don't sound as good as these others."

Again, you doubted your belief and you believed your doubts. It is time to break through doubting thoughts. It is time to break through to believing your beliefs and doubting your doubts.

I encourage you; do not pluck up in doubt what you have planted with belief.

People have talked themselves out of what could have been the most powerful inventions known to mankind.

Some of the greatest books are still unwritten or unpublished due to doubtful beliefs and/or talk.

Aren't you tired of giving life to your doubts? Isn't it time that you spoke death to your doubts and life to your beliefs?

Wow, I'm feeling this myself as I am breathing belief in you, my own belief is sucking the life out of my doubts! I'd buy another copy of this book myself, just to read this section!

If you purchased this book, you've received 10 times the price you paid for it already! That is why I am giving a 100% lifetime guarantee, which is almost never done with a book. I really believe this book will change lives around the world. Just imagine how much better it will be when you and a friend attend one of my life changing seminars or book me to speak for a group to which you are connected. When you feel my passion in person, you may never be the same again.

Now you can believe that, because I sure do!

A man once told me, "You are so convincing!" I replied, "No, I am convinced. Thus I speak from a place of conviction, which results in others being convinced. I am not in the convincing business, but rather in the conveying business, but when I convey with conviction, people tend to be convinced." Now it's your turn. From now on, I want you to believe your beliefs and doubt your doubts. Okay?? I didn't hear your answer, say it a little louder please. Okay? Now that's more like it, you are on your way to a Break Through or perhaps you've experienced one right this moment.

You Get What You Give

A dad was walking with his son through the mountains when the son fell and screamed out in pain: Ahhhh!

To his utter surprise, he heard the voice repeat somewhere in the mountains: Ahhhh!

A little curious he yelled, "Who are you?" He receives the answer: "Who are you?"

Now angered he screams: "Coward!" He receives the answer: "Coward!" He finally looks at his father and asks, "What's going on?"

The fathered smiled and said, "Pay close attention."

The dad screamed to the mountain: "I admire you!" the voice answers back: "I admire you!"

The dad screams, "You are a champion!" The voice repeats: "You are a champion!"

The boy looked bewildered so the dad explains, "most people call this an echo, but really it is life. It gives you back everything you say or do."

Our life is simply a reflection of our actions.

If you want more love in the world, create more love in your heart.

144

If you want more competence in your team, improve your competence.

This applies to all aspects of life; life will give you back everything you have given to it.

Your life is not a coincidence nor is it a mistake. It is a reflection of you!

Take responsibility (respond with ability) from this day, forward!

Helping Inner-City Youth to Break Through

It is time for me to break free!

CHAPTER 6

EGO

Ego stands for:

E - *Edging*

G - *God or Guidance*

O - *Out*

I Met God In The Morning

I met God in the morning
When the day was at its best,
And his presence came like glory,
Like a sunrise on my breast.

All day long, his presence lingered,
All day long, He sailed with me
And we sailed with perfect calmness
over many troubled seas.

Other ships were torn and battered,
Other ships were sore distressed,
But the wind that seemed to drive them,
Brought to me a peace and rest.

Then I thought of other mornings
With a keen remorse of mind,
When I too had loosed the moorings
With his presence far behind.

Now I think I've found the secret,
Found for a many a troubled way.
If you meet God in the morning,
You can have Him all the day!

- Ralph Cushman

Matthew 7:7, "Ask and it shall be given you, seek and ye shall find, knock and it shall be opened unto you."

A - *Ask*

S - *Seek*

K - *Knock*

It has been said that, "it is impossible to stumble if you walk on your knees"!

I do not know about you, but I do not want to edge God out, nor do I want to edge guidance out of my life. Fools run where angels fear to tread - why, because they will not listen to others who are wise.

Look at what is happening in our public schools. There was a day when prayer was allowed. They kicked God out when they kicked out the Ten Commandments. The only time young people can pray in school is when there is tragedy.

I tell people when they want to learn the martial arts, "Before I can teach you anything, I have to first of all break your knows; not your N O S E, but your K N O W S. It's not what you know that's going to hurt you, but rather what you think you know that's not so." It is what you learn after you think you know it all that really counts.

Many people have a know-it-all attitude—that ego that edges guidance out. It says, "Well, I know things, so why should I listen to others"? Many people could learn from a seminar, a book, or other people, but they do not primarily because they allow their ego to get in the way.

A man taught me years ago that everybody knows something that I do not know. Hence, I must probe and find out what they know. Thus, all men, women and children are my teachers.

Years ago I read this phrase and it has always stuck with me,

"The Beginning of greatness is to be little,
The increase of greatness is to be less,
The perfection of greatness is to be nothing."

I told my oldest son when he was young, "Joshua, one day you'll get to an age where you're going to think I don't know much. You're going to think I'm just an old man."

He was just a little boy at the time and he replied, "No Daddy, no Daddy, I love you. No Daddy, you are very smart."

I said, "Son, thank you. I receive that and you believe that now, but one day I'm telling you, you're going to get to be about 16, 17, or 18, and you may start thinking that I'm not so smart, that you know it all. Now just remember one thing."

And he said, "What's that, Dad?" I replied, "If you ever get to that point, remember, I'm a little smarter than you because I'm the one that told you, that you were going to get to a place where you thought you knew it all."

I am glad my son never really got to that point. He has been a very humble, extra respectful, and a very smart, powerful man. He recently made sergeant in the Marines. He, as all of my children, has made both their mother and me very proud to be their parents.

In all of us, something says, "I don't want people telling me what to do." Nevertheless, if it is something that can help us, embrace and receive words of wisdom from others.

In fact, I remember telling my son, "If you're like me, you don't like people telling you what to do. Figure out what they want you to do and do it before they say anything, then you will not have to listen to them tell you what to do, because it will have already been done."

The ego part of us just wants to figure and do things by ourselves. Most men will never stop and ask for directions, and they will drive all over town lost, but will not admit it. They waste valuable time because of their ego. Their wives or significant others will finally ask them to get directions.

They reply, "No, I think I know where I'm going now."

Here is an awesome truth I teach groups and organizations. "We may not have it all together, but together we have it all."

We would have more unity in our homes, we would have more unity in our churches, more unity in our businesses, etc. if, instead of having such big egos, we would learn to be united and work and learn one from the other.

When we break through our ego, we can each learn from the other and better ourselves.

I travel the world speaking at seminars, and I make sure I attend other speakers' sessions because I want to constantly learn. I don't know what I don't know.

I constantly have to suppress my ego, humble myself and learn from other people. The more I learn from others the better I get, because I can add what I learn to what I already know. Thus, I can become twice as smart. (smile)

Some of the greatest lessons I've learned are from people that weren't necessarily as smart as I view myself. I've learned great lessons from younger people.

I've learned lessons from people who didn't have it "all together" like I think I may have. But I'm a whole lot better person because of what I have learned from them.

I taught my sons and daughter, "If you'll learn what your mother and I teach you, then you have an opportunity of being such a powerful person. You will know what we know, plus the things that you have learned on your own, and that will give you the upper edge."

Isn't it something how we often listen to those whom we shouldn't, but don't listen to those that we should?

Teenagers often listen to their friends' lack of wisdom, and mess their lives up, instead of listening to their parents' loving wisdom that would save them much heartache. It is almost like saying, "No! I want to experience all of the heartache that you experienced for me, Mom and Dad. I want to get hit by a Mack Truck to see if it really hurts as badly as you say it does." Now, those who are fortunate enough to live through such an ordeal would readily write an endorsement or give a testimonial to what I am trying to get across to you.

At times men neglect the loving counsel of their wives concerning business matters. Wives can caution the husband about what she senses in an associate who lacks integrity, only for the husband to say, "Oh sweetie, he is a good man." Then, sadly enough the same man will follow unsound advice from their male friends to do things against their better judgment.

The male ego has caused many good men to overlook great wisdom from their wives simply because they want to try to prove that they are the man. A real man does not have to try to prove anything to anybody!

Months later the husband silently wishes he had heeded his wife's intuition concerning a lack of integrity or possible danger.

Can we all just stop and start doing the right thing—that is to follow good advice regardless of where or who it comes from?

An Acronym for Team is:

T	-	*T ogether*
E	-	*E ach*
A	-	*A ccomplishes*
M	-	*M ore*

But My Acronym for Team is:

T	-	*T ogether*
E	-	*E ach*
A	-	*A ccomplishes*
M	-	*M iracles*

Teamwork Makes the Dream Work!

It is time for me to break free!

www.JoinDrBreakThrough.com

CHAPTER 7

EXCUSES

Excuses are tools of incompetence used to build mountains of nothingness, and those that subscribe to them seldom amount to be anything.

- Anonymous

You have two choices. You are either going to make excuses, or you are going to make money, but you can't make both. By the way, look at your bank account. It will reveal which of the two you have been making.

You can either make excuses, or you can make progress, but you can't make both. For many years, I used my energy to make excuses.

One day it finally dawned on me, "I'm using my energy to make excuses, but it would make better sense to use my energy to make progress and money."

By the way, I made some great excuses in my past. In fact, I believed them and some other people believed them. I did not like the results. So, I switched and stopped using my energy to make excuses and I started using my energy to make progress and money.

I once heard my late friend, Anthony Clark (who was the World's Strongest Man), make a statement. "We were not born winners, nor were not born losers, but rather we were born choosers, thus you can choose to win."

You can choose to win once you stop making excuses and start making progress. My question is simple: Will you choose today to stop making excuses? When you stop <u>making</u> excuses, you will not have to <u>take</u> excuses.

One of the reasons many people take excuses from others is because they are planning to make excuses back to the same people. It is kind of like a safety net!

Once I committed to no longer make excuses, I called my team to let them know I would no longer take excuses.

Suddenly, they started making progress and money, and we were all further ahead.

You are liberated from ever having to take excuses if you decide today to no longer make excuses. What is your choice?

When you want something bad enough, you will make a way. If not, you will make an excuse.

If you are ready to commit to giving your all, to making no more excuses, you are about to experience a breakthrough.

Say aloud, "I am committed to use my energy to make progress. I am committed to use my energy to make money." By the way, the reason you need to stop making excuses and start making progress is that you will feel better about yourself.

Wouldn't you like to feel better about yourself? Well, of course you would.

Are you ready right now to make that commitment?

OK, say it out loud. "I commit to making money and progress." So be it! Sign below as a token of your commitment.

Unsuccessful people are champions at making and taking excuses.

Successful people are champions of making money and progress. Which championship results do you prefer?

Absorbing Two Punches in the Stomach

Certificate of Commitment

I _____ _____

here and now give up excuse making and taking and do solemnly commit to making money and progress this _____ day of the month of _____ in the year _____.

Now, have a witness sign here.

I _____ _____
witness this written commitment.

Now congratulate yourself for breaking through excuse making.

Yeah, you did it! You made the right choice!

CHAPTER 8

FEAR

I like these acronyms for fear:

F	-	*False*
E	-	*Expectations*
A	-	*Appearing*
R	-	*Real*

Or

F	-	*False*
E	-	*Evidence*
A	-	*Appearing*
R	-	*Real*

Many have a fear of the unknown.

Well, if it is unknown...

How do you know what or when to fear?

One of the most powerful CDs I have produced is called

Eat Your Fears Before Your Fears Eat You.

Usually, before I do that seminar I will swallow fire.

Now, that gets people's attention.

It also instantly kills bad breath. (smile)

Nelson Mandela, when taking office after being a prisoner for almost three decades quoted the following words by Marianne Williamson:

Our Deepest Fear

Our deepest fear is not that we are inadequate. Our deepest fear is that we are powerful beyond measure. It is our light, not our darkness that most frightens us. We ask ourselves, Who am I to be brilliant, gorgeous, talented, fabulous? Actually, who are you not to be?

You are a child of God. Your playing small does not serve the world. There is nothing enlightened about shrinking so that other people won't feel insecure around you. We are all meant to shine, as children do. We were born to make manifest the glory of God that is within us. It's not just in some of us; it's in everyone.

And as we let our own light shine, we unconsciously give other people permission to do the same. As we are liberated from our own fear, our presence automatically liberates others.

What do you fear…failure, rejection, others' negative opinions?

I want you to realize that fear and faith are twins. Fear is belief that the bad is going to happen. Faith is belief that the good is going to happen. You can only have one thought at a time, If you're going to believe something, you might as well believe that the good is going to happen.

What we fear will be attracted to us. What we have faith in we will be attracted to it. The fact that you believe you can have a breakthrough is what attracted you to read this book.

Fear will steal your power! I am sure that you have none to spare. 😊

Do you remember as a child fearing that a dog might attack you? The dog only responded to your fear and thus attacked. If you were like me, you were thankful for a parked car that you could jump on to get away from the dog.

Many people start a business fearing it will fail, and the fear that they have attracts failure to their situation. Many people are afraid that their health will break down, or that they will get cancer. Poor health responds to fear. Many people are afraid that their relationship will eventually break up, and unfortunately, that is what happens. The break up was attracted by the fear. Many of us believed that our relationship would not last because we came from broken homes. I could use more illustrations, but I think you get the point. What you are afraid of is in the process of being attracted to you, so please stop feeding your fear before it reaches you.

It may take a year, it may take five years, or 20 years, or (like in my case) 24 years, but the thing that you fear the most will eventually catch up with you. Give yourself permission to overcome your fear with faith. My first marriage of 24 years ended, as I feared it would, and while trying to figure out how such a sweet relationship could go sour it hit me, I secretly feared it would happen.

Job 3:25, "For the **thing which I greatly feared is come upon me**, and that which I was **afraid of is come unto me**." You see, Job was a rich man who had great influence, but in the back of his mind he kept thinking, "I'm afraid I may lose it all." Boy, was he ever right, because he did lose it all! He lost it all because he allowed the fear to live by feeding it, when he should have starved it to death with faith.

Different people fear many different things. Some people fear failure, others fear success, some fear rejection, some fear what others will say. Some fear what others may think about them. It does not matter what people think about you, as much as it matters what you think about yourself.

If you fear that people will not like you, people will respond to your fear and they will not like you, not because you are not a likeable person, but because of your fear.

On the other hand, if you have faith that people will like you, people will like you. They will respond to, and be attracted to your faith.

Fear says to me, "Dr. Stan, no one's going to purchase this book."

Faith on the other hand says, "Doc, people are going to purchase, and love this book. They will like it so much that they will buy another book and give it to a friend or family member, and say, 'You have to read this life-changing book. We must have Dr. Break Through come speak ASAP to our company, our group, our church, school, etc.' "

Faith says, "People will love this book so much that when they start reading it at night, they will stay up most of the night until they finish the book."

I will not allow fear to dominate my life, because I do not want those things. Instead, I am going to allow faith to reign and dominate. Somebody said, "Courage is fear that has said its prayers." You have to learn to break through your fears and break to the faith that tells you, "You can."

CHAPTER 9

LACK OF GOALS

You have to have something that you live for, something that drives you beyond yourself; something that makes you wake up in the morning, or occasionally keeps you up at night.

This book project is so special to me, and it has me reinvigorated in some areas. I anticipate hearing from many people concerning how this book has assisted them in having breakthroughs. I'm looking forward to hearing from you concerning how this book has helped you to experience at least one Break Through.

Tragedy comes when a person does not have any goals, when they have given up on their dreams and they give up on their hope. We use the word "hope" in a careless way. Hope is a well-founded, well-grounded expectation of the future.

I have never been hooked on dope, never even tried dope, but I am hooked on hope. Hope makes me live today as if tomorrow were yesterday.

Decide to break through to a goal or dream. Dream stands for

D	-	*Divinely*
R	-	*Revealed*
E	-	*Events*
A	-	*Awaiting*
M	-	*Manifestation*

Sometimes our dreams take so long that people often want to abort them and give up altogether.

People who have vibrancy in life are those who are living and not just existing. People with goals, dreams and aspirations become what we call the movers and the shakers.

You have to dream and you have to set some goals. A university did a study of graduates and only 3% of those studied had written goals. Years later, it was discovered that the 3% who wrote down their goals and dreams earned more money than the other 97% of the class combined.

Write down the area or areas where you want to experience a breakthrough, whether it is spiritually, mentally, emotionally, physically, in your relationships, in your business and/or finances. It is best to set a realistic date. I do not know why, I am just telling you it works. I cannot explain exactly how my vehicle works; I just put the key in and drive.

It is time for you to dream again. It is time for you to set some goals again. On the other hand, you may already have goals, you just need to establish higher goals.

It is time for you to stop existing. Animals just exist, but you are a human being. You were put here for a purpose. There is a divine purpose and reason for your existence. There is something that you have to offer the world, and if you do not rise to the occasion, the world will miss what it is you have for them.

"Nothing can resist a human will which will stake even its existence on the extent of its purpose." -Benjamin Disraeli

It is time for you to break through being average, start dreaming, and more importantly, make your dreams come true. Patiently work until your dreams come to fruition.

If you have not done so by now, set a date and write out an area that you want to experience a Break Through. The more specific you write, the better your chances of it happening.

Example 1 - Finish this book and have it published by March 4th, 2010, and on the best sellers list by August 2010 or sooner.

Example 2 - I will marry the woman of my dreams by the end of January 2010. She will be fair complexion, long shoulder-length hair, have a sweet soft voice, possess both inner and outer beauty and have an entrepreneurial spirit, and she will be crazy about me like I am about her. (This happened a year early, her name is Nadia)

Example 3 - I will make $100,000 or more in July 2010.

Goal setting, is telling the truth in advance. Write seven truths in advance you want to see manifested within 12 months.

1. _____

_____

_____

2. _____

_____

_____

3. _____

_____

_____

4. _____

_____

_____

5. _____

_____

_____

6. _____

_____

_____

7. _____

_____

_____

It is time for me to break free!

CHAPTER 10

LIMITING BELIEFS

Limiting beliefs keep multitudes of people from becoming their best. Often, I write the words "limiting beliefs" on a board to show the crowd that right in the middle of the word "beliefs" is a three-letter word called "lie." BELIEFS

Whenever our beliefs are based on a lie, it causes us to live a limiting lifestyle. Now, the sad thing about that is, 50% of our belief system is developed by the time we are 5, 95% by the time we reach 18. That means that the bulk of our belief system is based on our parents' beliefs, our society and the things that we were exposed to as young children.

I believe you need to wash your brain. Brainwashing is not always bad, but you need to wash your brain from the limiting beliefs you have embraced.

I used to subscribe to the limiting belief that because I was a young African American who grew up in the inner city with no dad, I could not be successful. Years ago a poem that I heard help set me free.

Dr. Martin Luther King, Jr. paraphrased William Cowper's Poem:

Fleecy locks and black complexion,
Cannot forfeit nature's claim.

Skin may differ,
But affection dwells in black and white the same.

Were I so tall as to reach the pole,
Or to grasp at the ocean at a span,

I must be measured by my soul.
The mind is the standard of man.

That poem help set me free, it gave me power; it helped me to break through a limiting belief. It dawned on me, it is not the color of my skin nor the texture of my hair, but rather what is in my head.

I teach people this principle, "What you put in your head and what you allow in your heart determine what God brings to your hand. If you want God to bring more to your hand, put more in your head."

Again, I want to honor you for reading this book with the commitment to implement this knowledge, thus allowing you to experience your Break Through!

Benjamin Franklin said, "Empty your purse (wallet) into your mind, and your mind will fill your purse (wallet) with gold."

Purchasing powerful materials like this book, and other materials, will fill your mind with powerful beliefs that will replace those limiting beliefs.

Many barriers are self-constructed (mental constructs), thus; they only exist in an individual's mind. Why limit yourself to non-existent barriers? Stop erecting barriers that do not exist!

- **Elephants**

Have you ever been to the zoo and wondered how a huge elephant is kept in place by a mere piece of rope tied to a stake?

Elephants begin training when they are babies. A huge chain is put around its leg and tied down to a powerful stake. That little elephant tries to run and gets to a place where it goes too far, the chain yanks his leg and he feels the pain.

The young elephant, full of energy and vitality, runs too far and feels the pain again. He does that repeatedly. They say after a few months, you can replace the chain with a piece of rope. The trainer drives the stake into the ground, and because of the elephant's memory, of the pain, he limits himself. That limitation, or belief that it's going to hurt, no longer exists but the elephant's greatest asset, his memory, now becomes his greatest liability (lie-a-bility).

- **Fleas**

The average flea can jump about 18 inches. Put a flea in a 10-inch jar with a lid on it. The flea associates pain with jumping 10 inches thus it trains its mind to stop just before it reaches 10 inches. After a month or so, you can remove the lid and the flea will never jump out of the jar. The only thing worse is the fact that the baby flea jumps even shorter because of his parents' limitations imposed on them. They just follow their parents' example.

- **Fish**

Piranhas were put in a tank with a glass plate that separated them from goldfish. After hundreds of unsuccessful attempts by the piranhas to get to the goldfish, the glass plate was removed.

Would you believe the piranhas starved to death even though a few goldfish bumped into them? Why? Because they were trained to believe they could not get to the goldfish.

- **Flat World**

It's hard for us to believe that people used to believe that the world was flat, thus they would not sail too far fearing they would fall right off the "Edge of the Earth."

- **Bleeding People**

President George Washington died because doctors, in an attempt to get rid of his "bad blood," put leeches on him. Needles to say, they now understand that life is in the blood.

How many of us have limiting beliefs? Some women think, "I'm just a woman in a man's world." Some people think, "I'm just an African American in a white man's world," or "I'm just a young man in an old man's world."

Whatever limiting belief you have, it's time for you to have a breakthrough.

Barak Obama helped change world history forever by winning the presidency of the most powerful country in the world.

Some people think, "I could never be happily married." That's a limiting belief.

Others think, "I could never raise good children." That's a limiting belief.

"Others can succeed, but not me."

Some people think, "I could never run a successful business."

Some have said, "I must have a man/woman in my life if I am going to make it."

Whatever your limiting beliefs are, understand this; they are all based on a lie.

You need to break through to the success that you desire and you deserve, and by the way - you do deserve it!

The level of your awareness of your self-worth will eventually determine the amount of your net-worth!

Some of the most beautiful women in the world do not believe that they are beautiful in spite of what others tell them, because in their youth they embraced a belief (belief) that they were not pretty.

The longer I live, the more I find other limiting beliefs that need to be rooted up like weeds in a lovely garden.

Take a moment and list some limiting beliefs that you may need to uproot.

(Examples - Money is the root of all evil.
     All rich people are snobbish.)

1. _____

_____

2. _____

_____

3. _____

_____

4. _____

_____

5. _____

_____

6. _____

_____

7. _____

_____

Keep Breaking Through Every Barrier

Can you guess what barrier I write on the 11th board before I break it?

CHAPTER 11

LOW SELF-ESTEEM

Most people, including strong men, have low self-esteem. In fact, the more boisterous a man is, and the more he over-accentuates his strength, the more likely it is that he is overcompensating for low self-esteem.

One reason some people suffer from low self-esteem is because they say things, but they do not follow through on them. Low self-esteem sometimes is tied into a lack of discipline or lack of follow-through. When you back up what you say with what you do, this increases your self-esteem.

Understand that without you ever having to do anything, God made you and God doesn't make any junk. So, that makes you special. There is no reason to have low self-esteem. Raise your self-esteem by understanding that you are somebody, and not just anybody, you are super special.

I'm so thankful for the people who were placed in my life that helped me develop a healthy sense of self-esteem, the people who esteemed me even when I didn't esteem myself. I want to pass some of that on to you at this very moment.

Someone said, "If you would have been the only person in this world, God would have still sent His Son just for you." That makes you special. In some cases, I tell people, "It's not really self-esteem you need; it's God esteem." When you recognize how much He thinks about you and the fact that He cares about you, that makes you someone very special. I love me so much that if I were not me, I would want to be me. People do business with people that they like, and people like people that they feel like them.

When you start liking and loving you, that will be one of the biggest breakthroughs ever!

**Dr Stan chopping 2 boards in mid-air with
a speed break**

CHAPTER 12

NEGATIVE TALK

MIT did a study and found that 83% of self-talk is negative. I often teach people to break through the negative talk of others, as well as their own negative self-talk, for example, "I can't, or that's impossible."

Learn to put a space between the "m" and the "p." Instead of saying, "Impossible," say "I'm possible." One of my mentors, by the name of Bill Bailey, once told me (during one of our many mentoring sessions) to "never use the word impossible." He asked if he could share with me why he made such a statement. I responded, "I'd love to know the answer."

He proceeded to share with me how his father told him it was impossible to put a man on the moon, and his grandfather told him the same thing. Yet, six months after Neil Armstrong walked on the moon, Mr. Bailey had lunch with him. So, he said, "Dr Stan, say things are hard or difficult but don't use the word impossible because it shuts your mind to the possibilities."

As I stated earlier, most of the things worth doing in this world were declared impossible by someone else before they were done. That's why you must cultivate a break through mentality and avoid negative talk.

Remember, it takes 17 positive comments to offset one negative, and the 18th positive comment puts you back to where you were before you heard the comment. That is almost unbelievable, but it helps us grasp the power of negative words!

Negative talk is something that diffuses and keeps many people from their success.

As I stated earlier, I like to refer to television as the *Electronic Income Reducer*, because the more people watch the less money they make. The more money people make, the less they watch television. I have one friend who got rid of his television until he was able to afford his own home theater complete with vibrating seats.

Examples of negative talk are as follows: "Well, this won't work, it never works. It did not work before, and it's not going to work now." You have to learn to break through the negative talk and break to the positive talk. Break to the right type of words, because words are powerful. Words are like seeds. When a seed (or word) is received/believed, it conceives and brings forth a harvest.

Negative words will produce negative results, whereas, positive words will produce positive results. Instead of being affected and utilizing negative talk, we need to get involved in positive talk. To some people, the glass is always half empty instead of half full. They're always talking about the things that go wrong, versus the things that are going right.

Negative talk has killed many dreams and has stifled many visions. It has left many people dead on the field of opportunity. I say it's time to break through the negative talk, even the negative talk and negative opinions of others. My good friend, Les Brown, says, "Don't allow someone else's negative opinion of you to become your own reality."

In a study of inmates, 90% of them were told by someone at one point in their life, "You're going to get locked up one day, and you are going to end up in prison."

I will never forget the day I got kicked out of school and came home. My mother looked at me and said, "Son, I'm doing the best I can. I am raising you and your brothers without a man helping me. You're about to break my heart, but I know one day you're going to make me proud of you."

When she said those words, "One day you're going to make me proud of you," that was a seed that she spoke and I received it. I believed it. It conceived and yielded a bountiful harvest. I am so glad that before she passed away, I had a chance to hear her say to me, "Son, I'm so proud of you. You have brought such joy into my life."

I will never forget the day she said, "I'm so honored and I'm humbled just to be able to know a person of your stature." I responded, "Mom, you are just reaping from the harvest that you sowed/planted years ago."

Negative talk or negative results, which do you choose? I hope neither.

Positive talk or positive results, which do you choose? I hope you choose both, because I did and the results are incredible.

Years ago, I developed this powerful quote: "We are reaping what we have sown by having what we have said. If you'd like a different harvest, get busy planting different seeds."

We need to plant powerful seeds in the lives of people around us. We need to plant powerful seeds in our own lives.

I like to say good stuff to myself. Instead of negative talk, we need to use good talk.

I often say to myself, "I like being me so much, if I weren't me, I'd want to be me."

Now for the last word/barrier that is perhaps, the granddaddy of them all.

This hinders more people than anything else imaginable and perhaps more than five or six of the other barriers combined.

Can you guess what barrier I am talking about?

Get ready, I am about to empower you to set yourself free!

About to Kick Through Procrastination

CHAPTER 13

PROCRASTINATION

I have saved the deadliest thing for the last, the thing that hinders more people from reaching their goals, dreams, or aspirations, the thing that hinders and destroys more relationships than anything else known to man. This thing has caused more lost opportunities, and it is responsible for some of the most powerful ideas going to the grave. It's none other than procrastination, which results in devastation. It is the assassination of your destination!

(Procrasti-<u>NATION</u>) I often share in my seminars that the largest nation of failures in the entire world are those who procrastinate.

The strange thing is we procrastinate because we are good people, and good people don't like to make mistakes. As children, we were excited, full of imagination, and willing to take chances, etc. Perhaps you remember sitting in school and thinking that you knew the answer, or at least you were willing to give it a try.

The teacher called you up to the front and you wrote your answer on the board only to have the kids laugh at you because you got it wrong. Maybe the teacher belittled you, and you said to yourself, "I'll never do that again." Maybe it wasn't you, perhaps it was your best friend or just another student that was belittled. You said, "I'm playing it safe, I'm not taking a chance of them making a fool out of me."

Remember, when you got older, got a job, and you found out that if you made enough mistakes you could get fired? This realization caused you to say to yourself, "I can't make any mistake. I've got to play it safe. I need my security." So now, you will not move until the perfect time or situation, but the problem is the perfect place, time or situation rarely comes.

So understand this, "You don't have to get it right, you just have to get it going, because once you get it going, you can always get it right." They say an airplane is off course up to 90% of the time but the pilot constantly makes adjustments. A car that's not moving is almost impossible to steer, but once it starts moving, it's easier to steer. The same applies to people, so just get in motion and make the corrections along the way and you will experience a breakthrough!

Break Through Time!

Imagine I'm on the stage with 13 people holding boards (12 of them facing you), representing the barriers that I will assist you in breaking through psychologically as I break them physically. Imagine my back is toward you, and the first two are broken simultaneously with a palm heel strike. I turn to my left and front kick: Comfort Zone. I use my right elbow to break: Disempowering Questions. I use my right hand to chop: Doubt. I use my left fist to punch through: Ego. I spin to my left and use the left elbow to blast through: Excuses. I use my left hand to do a knife hand strike to: Fear. I use my right hand and use a ridge hand strike to break: Lack of Goals. I use my head to break: Limiting Beliefs. I slide to the right and use my left hand to execute a Nika-tae strike to break: Low Self Esteem. I run to the right and jump up and with my right foot I high kick: Negative Talk. Upon landing, I turn to the right (facing the audience) and for the grand finale, I jump off of the platform and hammerfist strike with my right hand to explode thru Procrastination. All in under 9 seconds, the crowds jumps to their feet in applause, I bow in respect.

CONCLUSION

In conclusion, I want to tell you a story about a man who took his son to see the president of Morehouse College, Dr. Benjamin Mays. The year was 1944 and the man said:

"Dr. Mays, we've been friends for many years and my son is a good boy. He does not give me any trouble. He is a bright boy, he is brilliant, but he is missing something. He does not seem to have much drive. He does not seem to have any dreams. He needs some help. Can you help him?" Dr. Mays said, "I'd be glad to." Dr. Mays took that young man for a walk. He wrote powerful thought provoking words and said, "Son, I want you to read this every day with passion and vigor." The young man agreed. Daily the young man read the following words written by Dr. Benjamin Mays:

It must be borne in mind that the tragedy in life does not lie in not reaching your goals.
Tragedy lies in not having a goal to reach.

It is not a calamity to die with unfilled dreams,
But it is a calamity not to dream.
It is not a disaster to be unable to capture your ideals,
But it is a disaster to have no ideals to capture.

It is not a disgrace not to reach the stars,
But it is a disgrace to have no stars to reach for. Not failure, no, low aim, that is sin.

That young man became famous, I am sure you recognize his name, Dr. Martin Luther King Jr.

What a testament to the power of reading powerful words. I am concluding this book with my breakthrough declaration.

To hear my Break Through Declaration set to music, please visit my website www.FreeFromDrBreakThrough.com. I want you to commit to reading this every day for 30 days, and I promise you that it will change your life forever!

BREAK THROUGH DECLARATION

Wow! What a great day to be alive. Around me are bountiful opportunities. Before me are endless possibilities. Within me is the one who has infinite power, and behind me, well, who cares. I am succeeding in a great way and it is getting better day by day. Anything good that can happen will happen, and it will happen at the best possible time. I am exploding through barriers that at one time seemed insurmountable. I believe the impossible becomes possible with time, trust, talent, and endless trying. I will empty my wallet into my mind so my mind can fill my wallet. I am no longer bound by the limiting beliefs of my society, my parents or my past.

I am breaking to my destiny by breaking through every barrier that would hinder me. My mind is made up, thus circumstances are aligning themselves in my favor. I visualize vividly and verbalize veraciously, so I will soon actualize automatically. Instead of using my energy to make excuses, I choose to use my energy to make progress. I was not born a winner or loser, but rather a chooser. Thus, I choose to win daily. I will not be broken by adversity, but rather I will use adversity to help me break records.

I know that within any pain lies hidden power, and harnessed power can be used to create profits. Trouble never comes to a woman or man unless she brings a nugget of gold or good in her hand. I may look like a caterpillar, but I see myself as a beautiful butterfly flowing freely through the sky, like a rocket ship that seems to almost shake to pieces before it breaks through the earth's atmosphere. I will never go backward toward comfort and safety, but rather forward toward uncertainty, discomfort and growth. I will persistently pursue my passion in spite of any pain. I know that if I back down, I may break down. I will endure the test so that I may have a powerful testimony of how what once took so much effort is now done almost effortlessly.

I'm sowing powerful words, which are the seeds of success in my life and I gladly receive them. I will faith it until I make it by finding answers in the heart. Forsaking all, I trust Him. I call those things which be not as though they were. The facts are in, I've already won. I focus on what I want because I am no longer a seeing believer, but rather a believing seer. I no longer doubt my beliefs and believe my doubts, but I now believe my beliefs and doubt my doubts.

I forge ahead with positive force, and I will follow through to the end because I am a champion. I am a winner. I get results that last, because I take immediate massive action. I'm thankful that my God is raising a powerful people in prominent places, who are willing to use their wealth, influence and ability to help me break through to my wealthy place. The message that someone needs to hear the most, can only be received when they hear me. I will keep breaking through to become the best me that I can be, because from this day forward I am totally free.

Wow, do you feel the power of these words? Will you commit to reading them daily for 30 days to achieve a Break Through?

By the way, a Scott L., a 6-year-old boy in Texas, heard me read this Break Through Declaration, he resounded, "Dr. Stan, that's the coolest thing I've ever heard!"

It is your time to shine, because you, my friend, have the steps to break through to the success that you desire and you deserve. As stated earlier, I look forward to seeing you at one of my seminars. I look forward to hearing you on one of my tele-seminars. I look forward to having you as one of my coaching clients. DrBreakThrough@Gmail.com

Well, I want to show you how serious I am about assisting you with your Break Through. Please get your two tickets, altogether valued at $1,994, and hurry over to my site to reserve a spot for you and another person (seats are limited) at one of my life changing seminars. 1-800-518-2097

E-mail me and let me know how much you enjoyed the book and how it changed your life. Be sure to tell your friends to purchase their copy today! Would you like to know how you can make money and build a bigger team by selling my book? You can grab a free Mp3 that explains this powerful program. DrBreakThrough@Gmail.com Have a wonderful life!

AFTERWORD

Congratulations on finishing this amazing book. I am sure by this time you have already started to dramatically expand your life and manifest your BreakThroughs.

My advice to you now: Don't stop here.

Having read thousands of books, I know that many times after reading a book, no matter how transformational it may be, we have a tendency to slip back into old habits. When that happens much of what that we learned and much of the growth that we have experienced begins to wane. This is unacceptable! Personal development is not a destination but a process; a never-ending process. Now that you've come this far, you need to take the next steps to maximize the momentum you started and further solidify your BreakThrough or as Doc says in Chapter Six: Follow Through.

Fortunately, Dr. Stan provides you with complimentary opportunities for further development. The fact that you can dial a toll free number (866-704-4032) and take advantage of a thirty minute complimentary coaching consultation valued at over $250 is incredible! In addition, because Dr. Stan is completely dedicated to your continued success, you also can attend one of his all day Break Through trainings valued @ $997 (two tickets $1,994.00) absolutely free of charge. I'm confident that you are going to take advantage of this extraordinary offer while supplies last!

I don't know what your goals and dreams are but as a professional speaker, trainer and coach for over 40 years, I do know the power of the human spirit. I also know that the potential for personal growth expands exponentially with coaching and live meetings. There is simply nothing more powerful than learning life-changing principles in an environment of like-minded people!

So, if you are ready to take your Break Through to the next level, to intensify your results with Dr. Stan's coaching consultation and live trainings, and explode into your greatness, get registered right now. You'll be very glad you did!

Les Brown
Motivational Speaker, Speech Coach, Author
www.lesbrown.com

A Gift For You and A Friend!

Please enjoy this special bonus of two tickets each worth $997. ($1,994) value completely free of charge, all you have to pay is your own expenses to the meeting. Check my website often for time, dates and location.

Admit One   1-800-518-2097 $997.00

Your Break Through Is Guaranteed

www.DrBreakThrough.com   **Good through May 2012**

Please cut out and bring to seminar after registering.

Admit One   1-800-518-2097 $997.00

Your Break Through Is Guaranteed

www.DrBreakThrough.com   **Good through May 2012**

Please remember that you are responsible for all your meals, room and board, transportation, taxes, as well as any other expenditures.

Read what others have to say about Dr. Stan "Break Through" Harris

"My staff and I enjoyed having Dr. Stan Harris speak to us. He speaks with great energy, wisdom, experience and power. He personifies knowledge on Fire! He can move an audience to laughter, to tears, to the mountaintop! He is one of the most unusually gifted speakers that I have heard, and his message will be remembered for a very long time!"
Zig Ziglar
Sales Training Expert

"Dr. Stan Harris has that unmistakable charisma that puts him in the winner's circle. His unforgettable presentations demonstrate dramatically how to break through your mental barriers to achieve peak performance in the real world. I have shared the platform with him and been in his audiences. His reviews always mention the same four words: 'Life Changing, Smashing Success!'"
Dr. Denis Waitley, Author
"The Psychology of Winning"

"Dr. Stan Harris is one of my favorite people. He writes and speaks from the heart. His enthusiasm for life and empowering others is contagious, and anyone who hears him will never forget him or his message. Your life may never be the same again after hearing and experiencing his passion and zest for life!"
Charles Tremendous Jones
Author of LIFE IS TREMENDOUS

"I have been a mentor to some very powerful people and speakers like Jim Rohn, (who mentored Anthony Robbins) Les Brown, Larry Thompson, Willie Larkin, Rudy Revak, and many others, including Dr. Stan Harris. Dr. Stan Harris has an unbelievably powerful life message combined with a martial arts demonstration. He uses humor, wit and personal illustrations that produce results. He has the potential to affect an entire generation! We have shared the platform many times and he gets better every time I hear him! You owe it to yourself to hear and experience this man's awesome message!"

Bill Bailey
Success and Life Change Coach

"Dr. Stan delivers one of the most energetic and exciting presentations that I have ever been able to witness. His brick and board breaking demonstrations are the perfect metaphor for breaking through your fears and limiting beliefs. When Dr. Stan delivered our keynote speech at our last event, he created breakthrough results for our students that no other speaker has ever done. If you are looking for powerful results, Dr. Stan delivers!"

Matt Morris
Speaker, Trainer and Author

"Dr. Stan Harris is a *True Champion* - His heart pumps with Incredible Passion to teach others worldwide how to demolish their fears! Go ahead- Take advantage of his wisdom -today. You will be glad you did!"

John Di Lemme
Strategic Business Coach & International Speaker

"We have had many motivational speakers come to our events. Dr. Stan has been invited back to our events many times. He has figured out a way to have audience participation with motivation, inspiration and entertainment. If you want your audience on the edge of their seats, then you want Dr. Stan Harris! A speaker that your company will talk about for years to come! With Dr. Stan Harris, you don't just get a speaker, you get a champion!"

Bill Andreoli
President & CEO
Financial Destination, Inc.

"Dr. Stan has achieved at levels most only dream of, and if you follow his advice and example you, too, can become super successful -- super fast! He is a perfect example of what a human being can accomplish. He is a world-renowned champion black belt but more importantly, he is known for helping others achieve a black belt in life! He proves that success is available to anybody who wants it with all their heart."

Jack M. Zufelt
Author of the #1 best seller *The DNA of Success*

"Dr. Stan Harris will bring breakthrough results to ANY audience! His unique ability to captivate the mind while challenging the heart puts him in a league of his own. Any audience that is in need of empowerment, encouragement, or motivation, Dr. Stan is the man you need. He will move you to breaking through the ordinary to extraordinary. His message will enhance your life, I guarantee it!"

Johnny Wimbrey
Author, Trainer and Speaker

"Dr. Stan Harris is a powerful speaker and trainer who helps people to grow by helping them to overcome their fears and self limiting beliefs. He is a martial arts expert but more importantly he is a speaker who can help you to marshal the powers within and break through the challenges that are keeping you from living your dreams!"

**Willie Jolley,
Award Winning Speaker and Best Selling Author of "A Setback Is A Setup For A Comeback!"**

"Dr. Stan is one of the most dynamic, knowledgeable, and inspiring people I have ever known. His amazing presentations will help your people break through the barriers that are keeping them from being all they can be. You owe it to yourself to have Dr. Stan Harris speak at your next event. He will give your people an experience they will NEVER forget!"

**Ruben Gonzalez - Three-time Olympian,
Author of "The Courage to Succeed"**

"Dr. Stan Harris is one of a kind. His message is powerful, entertaining, and amazing. He will give you the ultimate experience and the ultimate gift to make you believe in you! He will lead you on an ultimate experience and you will believe you can break through life like he breaks boards. Powerful, Powerful, Powerful!"

**Barry Donalson,
President, MMG Marketing**

"I've had the privilege of hearing Dr. Stan speak on a private teleconference call as well as to interact with him personally and as a colleague. I've witnessed the impact his inspiration and excellence have had on those who hear him, and I've been personally blessed and uplifted each time I've spoken with him. Dr. Stan is a great gift and resource to his fellow man!"
Ben Lo, MD
Life & Wellness Coach

"Dr. Stan Harris' combination of passion, energy and authenticity is outstanding! He is so interested in helping you reach your goals and ambitions. You can't help but be helped when you get around him! Dr. Stan is the MAN!"
Coach Zev Saftlas
Life Coach

"I've had the pleasure of hearing Dr. Stan Harris speak many times. Every time without exception he has the audience engaged and exhibiting renewed excitement about their own potential. His presentation is powerful, his presentation method is unique and engaging, and his energy is contagious! I consider him one of today's great motivational speakers."
Larry Erdos, CEO Wave5, LLC

"Dr. Stan will help you break through whatever has been limiting you from accomplishing the success you deserve. His no-nonsense inspiring insights and his street-smart wisdom, along with your proper action, will allow you to live the life of your dreams."
Robert Butwin, Author of
Street Smart Networking

"As America's eXtreme Motivator, I can attest to the fact that Dr. Stan delivers a powerful message with eXtreme energy and enthusiasm. You can expect breakthrough in areas that you didn't even know were holding you back."

Patrick E. Alcorn
America's eXtreme Motivator
Author of *Paid on Purpose*

"Dr. Stan is a powerful speaker that will inspire you to take steps in the direction of your dreams. Passion and commitment are two things that give music to his communication. Get ready to be on 'Fire' as you listen to this powerful individual share his words of wisdom."

Ellie Drake
President, BraveHeart Productions

"Dr. Stan is one of the most electrifying speakers I've ever seen. He has that rare ability to connect with audiences of all ages, backgrounds & disciplines, mesmerizing them with his heartfelt stories and anecdotes. If you ever have the chance to hear his inspiring breakthrough messages, run...don't walk to be in his midst. But don't stop there. Put his teachings to work for you and expect great things to happen in your life."

Fran Harris,
WNBA Champion & Host of HGTV's "Home Rules"

"This is a masterpiece, simply amazing!"
Brenda Stroman
Entrepreneur and Teacher

"This message that Dr. Stan 'Break Through' Harris has for you is astounding and revolutionary, it can absolutely change your life. If you read, meditate and integrate this powerful teaching, your success and your breakthrough is guaranteed."

Ted Ciuba
Founder of The World Internet Summit
Author of The New Think and Grow Rich

"Dr. Break Through is an extraordinary author, speaker, and whatever else he puts his mind to. He is a masterful motivator and innovator, a genius at putting words together so as to get the greatest impact. Hear him speak, read his words, and I promise you, you will immediately let go of being tired and get inspired to have your sought after breakthroughs. I recommend this book to anyone who wants more from life, and wants it NOW!"

Joyce E. Barrie
Motivational Speaker
Personal & Professional Success Coach

"Dr. Stan Harris is truly a one of a kind individual. The delivery of his teachings and the experimental aspects of his trainings are spectacular. His dramatic demonstrations will truly alter your perception of what is possible... If you are seeking a Breakthrough in any area of your life, Dr. Stan Harris is the man to see... Your new found Results will become self evident... "

Go, Go, Go!!!
Jerry "DRhino" Clark
Human Potential Giant

A Breakthrough in your relationship will keep things sweet!

Nadia & Dr. Stan

HAVE FUN FINDING THESE KEY WORDS:

1. Forgiveness
2. Faith
3. Facts
4. Focus
5. Force
6. FollowThrough
7. Fast
8. BreakThrough
9. Systems
10. Abundance
11. Forgiven
12. Trust
13. Desire
14. Deserve
15. Belief
16. Break To
17. Formula
18. Wow
19. Done
20. I Can
21. Ask
22. Won
23. Now
24. Yes
25. Learn
26. Fix
27. Mom
28. Bee
29. Floor
30. Step
31. People
32. Grow
33. Free
34. Hit
35. Good
36. Rest
37. Boy
38. Action
39. Right
40. Truth

F	O	R	G	I	V	E	N	J	F	Z	F	E	K	S	A
O	A	D	R	K	I	N	W	H	O	F	A	C	T	S	B
R	R	S	O	F	Q	D	O	G	L	O	I	M	D	U	U
M	O	U	T	B	I	O	W	U	L	R	T	X	E	C	N
U	O	D	K	R	E	N	D	O	O	G	H	P	S	O	D
L	L	Q	A	N	E	E	G	R	W	I	A	D	E	F	A
A	F	I	E	K	W	S	G	H	T	V	Q	E	R	B	N
X	I	K	R	I	G	H	T	T	H	E	I	S	V	E	C
G	D	S	B	Q	E	F	H	K	R	N	C	I	E	L	E
E	M	O	M	Z	P	F	B	A	O	E	A	R	J	I	Y
E	Y	T	I	S	Q	X	V	E	U	S	N	E	O	E	E
R	P	E	O	P	L	E	S	R	G	S	I	Y	Q	F	S
F	S	Y	S	T	E	M	S	B	H	T	R	U	S	T	P
R	T	K	E	E	A	X	A	C	T	I	O	N	O	W	K
X	E	O	Q	R	R	S	M	N	P	O	Z	P	W	O	N
W	P	Y	U	S	N	W	B	O	Y	C	H	T	U	R	T

Answer Key on Website

Final Thoughts

What a man or woman believes, determines what they perceive, and what they perceive determines what they receive; consequently, what they receive will determine what they achieve!

We are standing together for your Break Through.

Be sure to order our soon to be releasd book titled:

Computer Love
How To Meet The Love Of Your Life Online

This was taken by Glamour Shots.
Take advantage of your FREE
8 x 10 Portrait
Certificate on page 201

Here's a copy of my business cards:

Order a copy of this life changing E- book that I Co-Authored along with 50 other Millionaires and Mentors!

You will get a huge bonus package worth $25,000.00! Time sensitive offer, hurry and order while supplies last!

www.WalkingWithTheWise.com/StanHarris

WHAT I LEARNED FROM
DR. BREAKTHROUGH:

_____

_____

_____

_____

_____

_____

_____

_____

_____

_____

_____

_____

_____

_____

_____

_____

_____

Dr. Break Through's Recommendation for Products and Services to help you Break Through

April 2010. I am still Breaking Through….how about you?!

www.DrBreakThrough.com

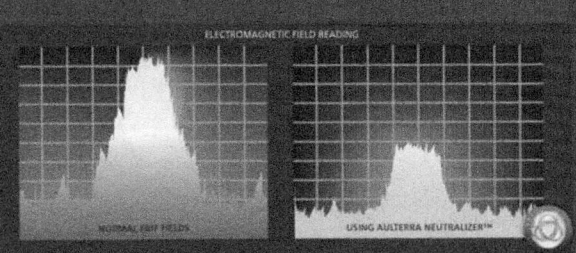

VALUED AT OVER $250!
THIS CERTIFICATE ENTITLES THE BEARER TO
ONE COMPLIMENTARY 30-MINUTE
BREAKTHROUGH
COACHING CONSULTATION
+BREAKTHROUGH BONUS REPORTS
TO SCHEDULE DR. STAN'S COMPLIMENTARY 30-MINUTE COACHING CONSULTATION
CALL 1-866-704-4032
FROM THE CREATOR OF
Guaranteed Breakthrough
Breaking Through Every Limitation
Ten Times Better
Millionaire Mindset
7 Steps to Success
Attack or Be Invaded
Magic & Mystery
DR. STAN HAS HELPED PEOPLE WORLDWIDE MAKE THE POSITIVE CHANGES THEY'VE ALWAYS HOPED FOR. NO MATTER HOW YOU WISH TO TRANSFORM YOUR LIFE, DR. STAN'S BREAKTHROUGH COACHING WILL HELP YOU BREAK THROUGH ANY LIMITATION!
COURTESY OF DR. STAN
POWERED BY PROSPER
one complimentary 30-minute BREAKTHROUGH COACHING consultation

www.DrBreakThrough.com

Fran Briggs is also Dr Break Through's PR Lady. Get a special discount when you mention you saw the ad in this book.
928-276-9093 franbriggs@aol.com

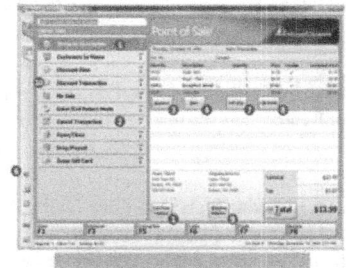

Dr Break Through has been a guest on this show many times.

7 Reasons Every Person Should Join
A Home Based Business! By Dr. Stan

1. **Tax Deductions**. Many people want to have as many Tax deductions as possible, owning your own business allows a lot of deductions that you otherwise could never take. Would you like to deduct part of your car mileage, phone, utilities, part of your mortgage etc? You can even pay your children for working with you in the business and deduct that as well. Get with a Home Business tax expert to get more details!

2. **To Have A Plan B**. Never put all of your eggs in one financial basket. It is wise to have diversified sources of income, especially with today's economic uncertainty. Having multiple streams of income is always a smart and safe plan.

3. **The Ability To Create Leveraged Income** J. Paul Getty the first Billionaire said I'd rather get 1% of the efforts of 100 people than 100% of my own efforts. We have all heard of CEO and CFO and COO but I like to empower people to become a CLO. CLO stands for Chief Leveraging Officer, why not leverage the work of others, and work as a team as you benefit each other.

4. **The Opportunity To Be Around Positive People**. You will meet some of the friendliest and most positive people when you are part of a home based business or free enterprise. Being associated with people who do what they love to do, and working with those that they like and trust, that is reason enough for me to join!

5. **The Opportunity To Create Freedom**. Through my business I now get to experience freedom. Freedom to be myself, and not some plastic person. Freedom with my time, because now I have created income that also allows me the opportunity to work my own hours etc. Many companies have paid vacations based on production and even luxury bonus cars and/or a housing allowance, wow!

6. **The Sense Of Belonging**. Everyone wants to fit in or have a sense of belonging. I have created friendships that will last a lifetime. I also like being where I am liked. Does that make sense to you?

7. **The Business Is Willable**. You can transfer or will your business, thus leaving a legacy for your family. Your offspring gets to benefit from all of your hard/smart work. You have worked hard enough, now it's time to work smart! Would you agree? Get started in a home based business today, you and your loved ones will be glad you did!

Start A Home Based Business

For A Free Coaching Session On How To Start A Successful Home Based Business Call:

Become A Hopeless Success

CONTACT INFORMATION

Dr Break Through LLC
Dr Stan & Nadia Harris
Download My Free App
DrBreakthroughApp.com

717-275-3508

DrBreakTo@Gmail.com
LadyBreakThrough@Gmail.com

www.JoinDrBreakThrough.com

Made in the USA
Coppell, TX
11 October 2024